Declare it Fearlessly

Published in Beaverton, Oregon, by Good Catch Publishing.
www.goodcatchpublishing.com
V1.1

Printed in the United States of America

Table of Contents

Acknowledgements

I would like to thank David Pepper for his vision for this book and for his hard work in making it a reality. And his missionary friends, thank you for your boldness and vulnerability in sharing your personal stories.

This book would not have been published without the amazing efforts of our project manager and editor, Debbie Allen. Her untiring resolve pushed this project forward and turned it into a stunning victory. Thank you for your great fortitude and diligence. Deep thanks to our incredible editor in chief, Michelle Cuthrell, and executive editor, Jen Genovesi, for all the amazing work they do. I would also like to thank our invaluable proofreader, Melody Davis, for the focus and energy she has put into perfecting our words.

Lastly, I want to extend our gratitude to the creative and very talented Jenny Randle, who designed the beautiful cover for *Declare it Fearlessly*.

Daren Lindley
President and CEO
Good Catch Publishing

The book you are about to read
is a compilation of authentic life stories.
The facts are true, and the events are real.
These storytellers have dealt with crisis, tragedy, abuse
and neglect and have shared their most private moments,
mess-ups and hang-ups in order for others to learn and
grow from them. In order to protect the identities of those
involved in their pasts, the names and details of some
of the people mentioned in this book have been
withheld or changed.

Introduction

Under house arrest, nearly two millennia ago, a man wrote to friends whom he loved with these words: "Pray also for me, that whenever I speak, words may be given me so that I will **fearlessly** make known the mystery of the gospel, for which I am an ambassador in chains. Pray that I may **declare it fearlessly**, as I should" (Ephesians 6:19, 20).

When the Apostle Paul bared his soul to the Ephesian church, he simply revealed the heart of every person whom God sends on missions to declare the good news of eternal life in Jesus. It's a heart set on fire with grace. A heart consumed with the Gospel. A heart that brings healing to the oppressed. A heart that when persecuted perseveres, when cursed returns blessing and when facing adversity overcomes. It is our hope that these authentic stories you are about to read will inspire you to live prophetic lives in this generation by declaring the Gospel fearlessly and to make disciples. As followers of Christ, we must embrace a mission posture with the courage to discover our voice. This is our time, this is our planet and this is our space in history to manifest intentional lives. If you crave a fresh demonstration for representing Jesus, then turn the page.

Church on the Wall
The Story of Jack McKee
Written by Richard Drebert

Mum loved to watch the flutists piping "Blood and Thunder" at the festival commemorating the Londonderry siege of 1688. She cheered the Lambeg drummers in the Apprentice Boys Parade honoring 13 Protestant youths who bolted shut the gates of Derry (Londonderry) against a Catholic king and his army.

"Surrender or die!" the king had commanded.

The apprentice boys' retort of "No surrender!" still echoes in the hearts of Loyalist Protestants in Northern Ireland today.

During the following 105-day siege, thousands starved to death inside the ancient walls of Londonderry, before British ships broke through a blockade to save them.

ॐॐॐ

In August 1969, at the annual Londonderry celebrations, street fighting broke out between Catholic Nationalists and Protestant Loyalists. Mum and her lady friends fled the chaotic streets of Derry, while radio and TV spread panic like an airborne disease. Northern Ireland's Protestant communities in Belfast feared that the Londonderry rampage signaled a national insurrection led by revolutionaries. Family men on our street corners and in local pubs armed themselves with baseball bats and iron pipes to fend off what we feared was an impending Catholic uprising.

Mum caught the night train to Belfast, while my dad, my three brothers and I paced on needles and pins. Very late, Mum made it safely home to Shankill Road.

On this same day, our Catholic neighbors on the Falls Road were arming themselves to defend against an expected pogrom. In the past, Catholic communities had been terrorized by groups of militant Protestant Loyalists.

Paranoia stole through our working-class neighborhoods like an evil Irish fog. Falls Road (the Catholic community) and Shankill Road (the Protestant community) ran parallel to each other. Side streets connected these two main thoroughfares like rungs of a busy ladder.

The day after the Londonderry riots, every side street or alley connecting the Shankill and Falls Roads became a no-man's land where neighbors hurled bricks at one another. Houses were stripped of refrigerators and furniture, and men and boys built protective barricades to separate Protestant and Catholic homes and streets.

Loyalist Protestants wished to remain part of the United Kingdom, and Nationalist Catholics wanted to break away from the UK to join Northern Ireland to the Republic of Ireland and form a "united" Ireland. In 1969, the violent season known as "The Troubles" erupted in Northern Ireland. Historians say The Troubles ended with the signing of the Good Friday Agreement in 1998, but ethnic bitterness still ferments among Protestants and Catholics today.

ॐॐॐ

During World War II, the German Luftwaffe had bombed Belfast, and Catholic and Protestant families worked together digging loved ones out of the rubble. Catholics and Protestants wore the same uniform and died on battlefields side by side all over Europe. After the war, soldiers were stitched back into our working-class fabric and segregated from the silk-handkerchief classes of Belfast.

My parents set down roots in a mixed community of Catholic and Protestants called Ballymurphy, and just like my Catholic chums, my belly growled for want of a meal sometimes.

Dad was a laborer in the Shankill, and after tending a boiler all day, he often spent the evening at a local pub. Mum went with him sometimes, but she didn't share Dad's penchant for hard drinking. I was a ginger-headed lad, too busy playing soccer or riding bikes to think about religion or politics. My Catholic mates and I "patrolled" Ballymurphy streets and dug bunkers in vacant lots as we pretended to be soldiers.

I never gave it a second thought when I ended up as the British officer — and my Catholic friends as the Germans. Even after a bloody world war, Irish Catholics preferred their children to play as Nazi storm troopers rather than side with those they perceived to be their arrogant, perennial landlords (the British).

By the time I was 8 years old, it was common to hear about neighboring Protestant families moving away from our community. Catholic hooligans sometimes shattered windows with bricks to intimidate Protestants, and it was becoming dangerous to raise a family in Ballymurphy.

"Hey! You! Are you Catholic or Protestant?" The sneering tone in the voice startled me.

I had wandered into a beautiful park on the Falls Road, where I sat listening to water burble into a giant sandstone fountain. A group of seven boys about my age suddenly hemmed me in.

I weighed my answer carefully. "I … I'm a Catholic," I said quietly.

The water fountain's gurgling seemed deafening as the lads' eyes bored into me. The leader of the rowdies suddenly snickered.

"Then say the Hail Mary three times …"

Barely hesitating, I nervously recited, "Hail, Mary. Hail, Mary. Hail, Mary!"

Even the most unregenerate Catholic knew the essential prayer of the Rosary: "Hail Mary, full of grace. Blessed art thou among women …"

Not me. My goose was cooked.

All seven ruffians took a turn pounding on me until my tears shamed them into leaving me alone. I never

Church on the Wall

forgot my beat-down at the fountain. In 1961, Dad moved our family away from the by-then predominately Catholic Ballymurphy.

From our new home at the "bottom" end of the Shankill Road, I ran the streets, as did my three brothers. Most of the time, God was the furthest thing from my mind as I spent my time with mates as wild as me — and loyal to Britain through and through. By the time I was 11 years old, a passion for gambling consumed nearly every moment I wasn't in school. Horses, dice, football games and especially card games, like poker and pontoon, held me in a vice-like grip.

"Deal me in, mates."

On favorite street corners all over the Shankill, men, boys and young women gathered to josh about or gossip and play card games. On tolerable days when the weather was mild, we sat on the bricks with little piles of our coins and bills beside us. We gambled for the pool of money in the center of our circle.

When I was 15, I quit school and went to work for a local brush manufacturing company. At 5 feet, 6 inches and 140 pounds, I swaggered with wiry ambition. My math skills and aptitude for administration helped me advance to "working dispatch," or keeping broom and brush orders flowing.

But if you were looking for Jack McKee at night, you'd find me around Brown Square playing card games for money, late and hard. All my weekly earnings went straight into the "pool" at my street corner casino. An angry restlessness carried me toward corruption and likely violence someday — until God tossed a monkey wrench into my gears.

"Come to our Crusader's meeting!" a man said, and my mates and I shivered as a cold wind swept away our excuses.

Laughing and jostling each other, several of us followed the man to the warm, friendly Elim Church on Melbourne Street, where, in the coming weeks, we checked out the girls, played cards on the sly and had fun disrupting their services. Our hosts may have despised our antics (like setting off fireworks inside the sanctuary), but no one kicked us out.

One frigid November night, as I sat for the mandatory preaching stint, God soaked into my empty soul, like water filling a sponge.

I suddenly "heard" the words the preacher spoke: about how God would not always have patience with a man. There would be a reckoning for my rebellious heart, and I knew that this unwelcome insight demanded my response.

"If you know that you need a Savior, raise your hand."

I shuffled past my friends to the front of the church to put all my cards on the table, once and for all. I was all in.

"I'm going to be a Christian," I vowed, and more than one of my friends, and some in my family, laughed.

My parents were not churchgoers, but neither were they unfriendly toward Christianity. Mum said she was

Church on the Wall

happy for me. Dad hugged me and said, "I give you two weeks, Jackie …" (That was in 1967, and both Mum and Dad committed their lives to Jesus before they died.)

Sunday had always been my best gambling day in the Shankill, but I tucked my Bible under my arm and nodded to my cohorts as I passed them on the street corner. They stood up and stared for a few seconds, like I led a funeral march.

"Oy! Joshua! Where ya' headed?"

"No, he's *Moses*, with his big Bible!"

I could feel the back of my ears burning as their laughter faded away.

Later I learned about the two men my mates associated me with — God's powerful commanders, Joshua and Moses — and I accepted their jibes as accolades. I often stopped by my old gambling corner to see mates, but I never cut a deck for money again.

I was still spiritually rough as a cob while attending Crusaders youth meetings and regular church. But God captured my heart with his word and guided me to "devotionals" that shaped me for a lifetime of spiritual brawls with the devil.

David Wilkerson loved the gang members that he confronted in the back alleys of New York. His life and the stories about young men and women Jesus rescued from drugs and corrupt street life stirred my own love for Shankill kids chained by addictions and bitterness.

Twelve Angels from Hell. The Cross and the Switchblade. Run, Baby, Run …

Declare it Fearlessly

Did I have the courage to love people and serve God like David Wilkerson?

My test would soon come after I encountered savagery that surpassed anything I had read in *The Cross and the Switchblade.* On the streets of Shankill, the odyssey of God's miracles seized my life and continue to grip me to this day.

୭ଚ୭ଚ

The day after Mum returned home safely from Londonderry, much of Belfast was ablaze with sectarian fires, violence and death. No one stood on street corners for games and gossip anymore, and tools became weapons in the hands of our tradesmen. Men with wooden baseball bats (built in a brush factory where many of us worked) guarded gaps in barricades, determined to keep the enemy from invading our neighborhoods.

Police officers, hopelessly outnumbered, stood between the enraged factions. Bandaged and limping cautiously through Catholic and Protestant districts, they tried in vain to control the mobs. Families along the Shankill and Falls Roads felt abandoned by authorities. If laws still existed at all in Northern Ireland at that point, they were in the hands of individuals.

Courage or cowardice marked a man for life on the Shankill.

The interface areas (Catholic/Protestant flashpoints) seethed with crowds, mainly of men — young and old — concerned with defending communities. I had been taught

Church on the Wall

at my Elim Church to "overcome evil with good," but at 17 years old, my emotions pursued an instinct to protect my family. My father and brothers grabbed weapons and manned barricades to defend the Shankill, and so did I.

Men with military backgrounds, and respected individuals in our community like my father, filled leadership roles. I stood with my dad and brothers, hoping that God would honor my decision — I believed that it was either *them or us.* To my shame, I launched into the street fighting, as caught up in defending my territory as any gang member loyal to his colors in the alleys of New York.

During the first bloody days of anarchy, our religious/ political borders were clearly defined by the hodge-podge of barriers stacked on streets. Women and children were taken and guarded in church sanctuaries far from the fighting, until the initial mob violence ebbed.

Within a week of The Troubles, Catholics and Protestants began trading bats for carbines and assault rifles. Mobs dwindled, and snipers suddenly owned the deserted streets.

The government sent in British troops, and they marched down the Shankill Road amid our hopeful cheers and shouts. With fixed bayonets and helmets glinting, hundreds of soldiers tried to take control of Protestant and Catholic areas. Troops erected gun placements at flashpoints — but immediately seemed paralyzed between the warring sects: Stones and bricks from rooftops and balconies rained upon them indiscriminately!

Declare it Fearlessly

Within a matter of months, men at pubs were laughing at the impotence of the British, who seemed unable to adapt to a guerrilla war. The Irish Republican Army had assumed a leading role among Irish Catholics and now held positions at significant crossroads along the Falls Road. Masked men with Armalite AR-18s (obtained from IRA supporters in the United States) strutted like peacocks or crouched in pillboxes, laughing in the face of the British.

Shankill men, like my father, realized that the British strategy for quelling the violence had failed and worried that the troops might pull out — leaving us as prey to merciless IRA Nationalists. At homes and pubs across the Shankill, men gathered to form up the Ulster Defense Association, an underground league dedicated to keeping our community safe. If the Brits didn't have the stomach to deal with IRA thugs, then our UDA would — at least that's what we believed.

I watched stockpiles of carbines and automatic weapons being ferried from house to house, and I knew that an all-out guerrilla war brewed strong and unrelenting. Men whom I looked up to called themselves freedom fighters, but British security forces would kill an armed UDA Loyalist as quickly as they would an IRA rebel.

I asked myself, "How can a Christian be part of a covert terrorist group — even if it exists for the right reasons?"

I anguished over finding a legitimate means to honor

my family, my country and God, and I decided the best way for me was to become a part-time soldier in the Ulster Defense Regiment, where Ulstermen loyal to the Crown determined to protect civilians — whether Protestants or Catholics. As far as UDR soldiers were concerned, terrorists of *any* ilk stood squarely in our sights.

                        ❧ ❧ ❧

The night that dark-haired Kathleen fixed her eyes on me — in what I believe was a vision from God — she owned my heart. I had been praying alone, asking Jesus for a true-hearted girl, and suddenly her face brightened my soul, like the sun christening the Mountains of Mourne.

And I wasn't the only one who thought we were a good match. A wise youth leader gave me a job helping keep the Elim church books and then asked Kathleen to assist me. Kathleen and I began dating while she was still in school, and we made wedding plans after she graduated.

Kathleen's father was a strong Loyalist, too, skilled in repairing aircraft for the RAF. My beloved was 16 months younger than me, and during my restless teens, Kathleen had been growing into a fine Christian woman — very close to where my family lived!

While Kathleen and I dated, I followed in my father's footsteps, hopping from one job to the next between my assigned military duties. I landed daytime employment at a warehouse on Northumberland Street, scheduling tile and carpet shipments, which was a stone's throw from a British checkpoint separating Catholic and Protestant neighborhoods.

After The Troubles began, the British government erected a series of fences between the Shankill and Falls Roads, to deter random murders and bombings. Originally this fence was built to last about six months, but our "peace wall" became a permanent 20-foot-tall palisade made of brick and steel and several miles long. Gates are still locked tight at night.

In 1971, most major Shankill interfaces were manned by British or Ulster Defense Regiment soldiers with automatic weapons.

"Ya gotta see this, Jack! There's a guy outside hauling a big 'Jesus' cross on his shoulder. No joke!"

I dropped my paperwork on the desk and trotted outdoors to glimpse a meaningful (and prophetic) sight that has resonated in my heart for more than 40 years. A hippie-looking man with long blond hair and a black leather jacket shouldered a wooden cross. On it, John 3:16 was inscribed, and I greeted Arthur Blessitt as he hauled the emblem of God's love right down the middle of the street toward the British checkpoint leading to Falls Road.

I stared in awe as the soldiers dragged back their formidable barbed-wire barrier and allowed Blessitt to pass to the perilous Catholic side of Belfast. Minutes later he was confronted by hooded IRA members bearing automatic weapons, but after a tense discussion, he walked on, unmolested. It was the last I saw of Blessitt for several years. Blessitt returned to his home in Los Angeles and continued on a journey to carry the cross around the world.

Arthur Blessitt's dangerous "cross walk" on the Shankill and Falls Roads breached a wall of bitterness that had been passed from generation to generation. The sudden appearance of the empty cross reminded people that Jesus had faced terror and defeated death. Because of Christ's resurrection, every individual in Northern Ireland could know true and eternal peace, no matter what personal tragedy he or she encountered on earth.

And no one was more challenged by seeing the cross on our streets than me, 19-year-old Jack McKee.

∿∿∿

"Jack, sometimes I worry that we'll never see our wedding day," Kathleen confided one evening.

And I wondered about it, too.

About five months after I joined the Ulster Defense Regiment, a member of my unit (and neighborhood friend), Private Bobby McComb, was kidnapped.

After socializing with a young woman, Bobby had escorted her home, then walked through Protestant neighborhoods, hoping for a taxi. Paramilitary members abducted the young soldier, unarmed and out of uniform, from the Shankill streets. The terrorists burned the sign of a cross into Bobby's back, and their hot iron left a merciless signature beside the cross: I-R-A. Bobby's agony ended when a terrorist fired a bullet into his head.

Terrorists targeted UDR soldiers for abductions more often than civilians to instill a gnawing dread within our ranks — and in our families. Most of us in the UDR made a promise to ourselves that we would NEVER be taken alive by IRA terrorists. My own "pact" was flexible according to circumstances — and I kept it secret, between God and myself alone.

A month before I married Kathleen, I confronted this life and death decision when an IRA terrorist — bold as brass and unmasked — drew down on me with a pistol. I had been walking along Crumlin Road, off-duty and out of uniform, and I instinctively grabbed for my sidearm that wasn't there. Bobby's fate flashed through my mind, and I dashed away like a greyhound.

My assailant was only 30 feet away, and five bullets wailed past my ears, never so much as grazing my collar. If I had ever needed proof that Jesus set apart Jack McKee for his purposes, I believed I had my confirmation that October evening.

తతతత

Mum and Dad had adored Kathleen since her days skipping rope in Brown Square, and her parents respected me. I married my sweetheart in November of the same year that I joined the UDR.

In 1972 I was a proud soldier, a young Christian who

had answered my calling to save lives. My wedding was a milestone of joy in my life, and Kathleen's faithfulness and love became God's anchor that held me from drifting into bitterness after seeing the atrocities committed by Protestant and Catholic terrorists.

Just three years before our wedding, our families stood together as smoke from burning homes brooded over the Shankill. Now Irish Republican Army agitators stoked the fires of hatred even brighter and more deadly. IRA terrorists were growing more and more proficient at planting bombs, and their objective was to bring the Northern Ireland economy to its knees.

As a part-time soldier, I drove an armored Land Rover for my unit every night, searching for terrorists. It was "clean" duty for me — preferable to mounting attacks of reprisal, like the UDA had begun doing by then. My father had read the handwriting on the wall and quit the UDA, before they began justifying bombings that killed Catholic civilians.

My unit focused on protecting Belfast's industrial areas, especially electrical utilities. Each patrol area had designated code names, like "Green One," and we stood watch at various power plants to thwart bomb attacks. If an electrical grid went dark, terrorists and criminals wreaked havoc in that community.

Green One sprawled atop a mountain overlooking Belfast, and I pointed my rifle barrel downhill, slowly scanning the gate area with a night scope. Amid the green fluorescent glow from trees and fencing, a white light squiggled in my crosshairs.

"I've got somethin', Sarge …" Quickly my warning climbed the command ladder and back down to men stationed at the bottom of the hill.

Within minutes, our soldiers apprehended three IRA terrorists who were placing a bomb. The British soldiers who relieved our unit in the wee hours of the morning would have been blown to pieces when they opened the gate.

Oh, Lord Jesus, thank you.

I had a small part in saving lives that morning.

చచచచ

"Does that car look a bit heavy to you?" I asked my colleague in the seat beside me.

We were patrolling the streets in our Land Rover retrofitted with steel armor for protection against IEDs (improvised explosive devices). We peered through one-and-a-half-inch-thick bulletproof glass, installed to protect us from burning petrol bottles heaved from balconies.

The suspect car squatted drunkenly on a street lined with a dozen shops, and folks casually milled from one to the next. After I parked the Rover, we trotted in and out of the shops asking questions.

"I don't know whose car it is, but come to think of it, I did see two men get out and leave in another car."

"And you're still HERE?" I said, herding everyone out the door.

Church on the Wall

In a matter of minutes, our unit had secured both sides of the street, and shoppers and shop owners stood a block away watching us.

The British bomb disposal unit arrived, and one soldier dressed from head to toe in a flexible armored suit approached the car. As if on cue, the 1,000-pound fertilizer bomb detonated. The bomb expert stood only 15 feet from the loaded trunk, and the explosion tossed him through the air like a ragdoll. I curled up under the Land Rover as shrapnel (car fragments, brick chips and wood slivers) filled the air.

Unbelievably, the British bomb expert wasn't seriously injured, but every shop on the block was leveled.

Once again, God had protected us as we saved lives.

ৡৡৡ

Kathleen and I had been married three and a half years when she gave birth to our first child, a son we named Jonathan David, to honor my friend David Douglas. Davy came straight from Young Offenders Institutions to work with me as a helper during my day job. After night patrols with my UDR unit (and a few winks of sleep), I drove a truck for a furniture company to make ends meet. My new teenage assistant, Davy, was great on the other end of a couch or dining table during deliveries.

Davy's mother had died of cancer when he was in lockup, and I became his big brother, giving him space on our floor at home to sack out whenever he needed. He often stayed with us after work, since he lived clear across Belfast.

"Tell me again, Jack."

A Bible verse that his mother often quoted wrapped him in a shawl of consolation as he dealt with personal struggles in his life.

"For God so loved the world, that he gave his only begotten son ..."

I'd quote the verse, John 3:16, then explain, "God the Father loved you so much, Davy, that he sent his one and only son to die for you. And if you take him into your heart and serve him, you'll go to be with Jesus when you die."

For several months I worked with Davy, and every few days he would ask me, "Can you say the verse again, Jack?"

I'd lovingly quote it one more time, hoping that he might open the door of his heart, once and for all, and let Jesus fill his emptiness.

I wasn't happy when Davy lost his job with us and ended up at another company in the Shankill. He found work with a warehouse manager who was also a leader in the UDA. Davy's father had been a member of another Protestant terror group, known as the UVF (Ulster Volunteer Force), and I feared that Davy might be drawn into terrorist activities.

When I heard that Davy and the manager had suddenly abandoned their delivery truck on a street in the Shankill — likely kidnapped — my heart nearly burst with grief. Kathleen and I prayed over Davy's picture every night for months, until the authorities finally dug up two bodies: Davy's and his foolish manager's.

Davy's new boss had allegedly been skimming funds from the UDA, and members of the UVF had been tasked to punish him. Davy had been killed by the very organization in which his father had served. For Jack McKee, any hint of sympathy for Protestant paramilitary organizations like the UDA and the UVF died with Davy. An unseen evil had penetrated the souls of men and women in Northern Ireland, seducing them to kill their own young. I detested this evil *and* the terrorists who committed murder and called it "justice."

No power on earth could rescue Northern Ireland from the scourge of hatred flowing in the very DNA of Catholics or Protestants. Only one person could create a new heart — the same God who had set his seal of survival on me when I faced death patrolling the streets of Belfast — *Jesus.*

Not the "Jaysus" my mates invoked when cursing at snipers on rooftops. But the one who saved *me* in ways too deep to express with words.

In 1977, I laid down my arms and returned to civilian life, with Christ as my sole commander. I had been in the Ulster Defense Regiment for five years when Kathleen and I sold our possessions and moved to England for ministerial training at Elim Bible College (now Regents Theological College).

After two years, I graduated, and the Elim church

administration assigned me to pastor Elim Pentecostal Church in the farming community of Rathfriland, County Down. We loved the people, but I was a fiery inner-city boy from Belfast, lacking the gentle, unhurried disposition common to country folk. After two years, Ballysillan Elim Church needed a pastor, and I jumped at the chance to return to our old Shankill community.

The same neighborhoods I had patrolled as a soldier, I now visited as a pastor, and all the families up and down Shankill Road quickly became as precious to me as my own kin.

Our Ballysillan church membership grew, and we knocked out walls to expand the facilities. Our worship seemed to touch the very throne of God — but a strange restlessness kept me from setting down roots.

We had two wonderful daughters, Chara and Paula, and Jonathan was growing up to be a fine Christian man. Kathleen was as active in our growing ministry as I, yet I didn't feel content in my role as a pastor/teacher. Every day I yearned to be out of my office and on the Shankill streets, reaching out to young men and women who were dying without knowing Jesus.

Young people idolized the violent, amoral Shankill paramilitaries that preyed upon them. These organizations had mutated into mafia-style drug and racketeering businesses. Contractors, flower shops and pubs paid for their "protection," and drug money lined the brigadiers' pockets. The IRA, too, now acted as a powerful syndicate, as brutal as any mafia organization in the world.

Church on the Wall

No man dared challenge the overlords of the Shankill and Falls Roads: on the Protestant side, the UDA, the UVF and others; on the Catholic side, the IRA and IPLO. Young people were actively recruited by Loyalist or Nationalist paramilitaries who doled out fast cars, weapons, drugs and street status based upon a "soldier's" willingness to obey orders.

During my first seven years pastoring the Ballysillan church, my fiery indignation sometimes fizzled to despair. Jesus stood with strong, outstretched arms to care for families and youth, yet thousands upon thousands preferred to stay in their deadly cesspool rather than come to church.

Jesus said that he was *seeking* to save — and I concluded that Belfast would only see revival if Christians dared to enter the cesspool where the world lived. Sunday after Sunday, I preached it: *Nowhere in the word of God is the world commanded to come to church. But the church is commanded to go into the world and preach the Gospel.*

I began to respond to the same burning call of God that David Wilkerson experienced when he reached out to the gangs in New York. Like Arthur Blessitt, I hoisted a burden of love upon my shoulders — and stepped into the streets.

"He's on the run, Kathy. He needs a place to stay ..."

My wife smiled, nodding. She gathered up blankets and handed them to me so that I could make the fugitive's bed on the living room floor. Now, when members of the

UDA or other paramilitaries fell out of favor, they sometimes came to me for help. Often they were marked for a bullet, and I tapped resources to pay their way out of Northern Ireland for a new start.

I prayed that our unsaved Shankill neighbors were sensing that God had "moved out" of the church building and into the streets. Through our new evangelism teams, Jesus was on his way to find them. But the deeper that we patrolled in the devil's territory, the more dangerous it became for all of us.

৵৵৵

In 1989, while I still pastored at the Ballysillan Elim Church, God helped me raise funds to buy an old cinema to open a Youth and Community Outreach Center. One of the paramilitary groups was bidding on it, too, and offered double the price. Then another cinema company slid in its bid at three times my offer. The sellers sold it to me because they liked our agenda to help at-risk youth.

In January 1992, after nearly 10 years as pastor of the Ballysillan church, I tendered my resignation. In my soul I felt God's urging to give up the Ballysillan pulpit and reach out to the Shankill youth in a more focused and tangible way.

It had taken me three years to fund and refurbish the interior of our new facility, and my dream was finally becoming a reality. Government agencies had endorsed our 12-week interventionist program that we called

Higher Force Challenge, in which we gave at-risk youth safe harbor away from the streets.

In just one month I would hand over keys to a new pastor, and I faced a long, hard road ahead, opening rapport with a street community shredded by violence and bitterness. Little did I know that God planned to catapult me into the public arena. And in an angry burst of confusion, I would question if my vision to build a youth center was God's will at all.

I led Andrew Johnson to Christ when he was 11 years old. I baptized him at 14. I buried him at 17.

Like myself at about his age, Andrew's commitment to Jesus hadn't wavered. He was one of our Shankill kids who had a bright future — one of my blessed success stories.

The night that Andrew was shot, the police knew that a Ballysillan Protestant in the Shankill would die. Authorities had sent word to pubs and shops that IPLO (Irish People's Liberation Organization, an offshoot of the IRA) would be stalking Shankill to retaliate for the shooting deaths of five Catholics on Ormeau Road. No one had been charged in the killings, but everyone assumed that the shooters were Protestants. At his home, Andrew had wept as he watched a television account of the horrific murders.

He had turned to his mother, grief-stricken, and said, "Why? Why do people kill in the name of Protestants? These people don't represent us!"

The IPLO clamored for Protestant blood. Two masked

terrorists, not much older than Andrew Johnson, burst into a video store where he and another worker stood behind the counter. Andrew quickly shoved his colleague to the floor as the killers opened fire. Andrew saved the young woman's life, but he took two bullets to the chest before the assailants ran back to a getaway car.

I had just arrived home after ministering to a woman who was dying of cancer at a local hospital, when Kathleen met me in the driveway, crying.

"It's Andrew. He's been shot dead, Jack."

A thousand thoughts collided in my head as I drove to the video store where Andrew had been working. Police were trying to direct traffic away from the crime scene — located a few hundred yards from our church doors.

Someone told me tearfully, "He should have been at the youth meeting! But he was covering for someone who needed the night off."

Why Andrew, Lord?

Starting in my childhood, so many friends and neighbors had been murdered by paramilitaries — and my emotions gathered in a storm of rage. Inside my Renault, head on my steering wheel, I poured out every drop of pain for God to hear.

"Lord! You could have stopped this murder! Why didn't you? This boy was on track."

Through my tears I saw a man approaching me, and my friend and associate pastor spoke through my closed window. In a few moments, his kindness brought me back to myself.

Church on the Wall

I had to go see Andrew's mother right away. The boy was her only son …

On the day of Andrew's funeral service, Ballysillan Elim Church opened its heart and doors to the whole grieving Shankill community. Belfast police officers — Catholics and Protestants — helped us secure the blocks around the church. We had expected a crowd — but not *10,000 people*!

Loudspeakers set up in the street broadcast Andrew's eulogy to the throngs gathered there. As his mentor and pastor, I validated his innocence and denounced *all* terrorist groups. I implored the members of Protestant paramilitaries to stand down, saying, "Don't even think about taking anyone's life on Andrew's behalf!"

I paused — *feeling* murmurs slice through the crowd like a blade: "Right, Jack. Sure …"

అలు అలు అలు

After Andrew's funeral, I questioned if I had interpreted God's will for me to dive into spiritual "hand-to-hand combat" on the Shankill streets *rightly*.

Within three weeks, the three young men involved in Andrew's murder were shot and killed in retaliation. Belfast had entered a new era, writhing in greed and ruthlessness that I had never seen. Young men and women wanted a share of wealth and power held by Loyalist or Nationalist commanders, and fewer were joining paramilitaries to defend their Catholic or Protestant communities anymore. They craved the "bling."

Chicago-style crime syndicates ruled the Shankill and Falls territories now — and after Andrew's very public funeral, I stood in their crosshairs.

Jesus said, "Very truly I tell you, unless a kernel of wheat falls to the ground and dies, it remains only a single seed. But if it dies, it produces many seeds" (John 12:24).

I emerged from my grief and shouldered the cross again, more dependent upon God's Spirit to guide me than ever before. The media's saturating coverage of Andrew Johnson's death and funeral launched me into a blinding, uncomfortable spotlight. But it also served God's purposes. I became a "voice for the voiceless."

We called our ministry New Life Fellowship, and our worshipers and workers included former paramilitary members, street evangelists and local families. We met in the top-floor room of the old cinema, and our unconventional venue grabbed the attention of young people.

God also supplied Kathleen and my children a beautiful new home, and we moved there, just a year before the Ulster Defense Association sentenced me to death.

When the Semtex bomb detonated at the counter of Frizzell's fish shop, our old cinema shuddered, like it was

Church on the Wall

broadsided by a sudden wind gust. Sixty youth and children's ministry workers from several churches sat together upstairs for training at our New Life Fellowship, just 100 yards away from the blast.

Rushing downstairs, we stepped outside into a crisp, bright autumn afternoon, staring at the smoky havoc down Shankill Road. I hurried toward screams, where people staggered over dust-covered rubble. John Frizzell and his daughter were Baptist born-again believers. They died in the blast, along with seven others, including my 14-year-old daughter's friend Leanne.

The fishmonger's shop was completely torn out of a solid row of businesses, and it lay in helter-skelter mounds of brick, splintered lumber and jagged steel. Ambulances carried away the bodies they could find, as well as people wounded by the odd-shaped masonry, plumbing and roofing "shrapnel" flung in the blast radius.

All night, police, firemen and ambulance drivers dropped body parts into plastic bags as they worked to find remains.

We continued to pray for survivors throughout the night. One of them was the terrorist — a 19 year old who had assisted the one who prematurely set off the time bomb. Their target had been leaders of the UDA who met on Saturdays in the upper story above the fish shop — but none of that terrorist group was in the building at the time. The UDA went into high gear using the emotional fallout from the bombing as a recruitment tool on the streets.

Declare it Fearlessly

ॐॐॐ

Soon after the Shankill bombing, I stood before a bouquet of microphones and television cameras, my ire held in check by God's Holy Spirit alone. I despised the IRA terrorists for the atrocity, but I believed that Protestant paramilitaries were the magnets that invited such an attack.

Neither terrorist faction could vanquish the other — but through fear and violence they intimidated and controlled the people like vassals. I took careful, deliberate aim at ALL the paramilitaries. As the cameras zoomed in closer, I condemned the IRA terrorists who killed nine absolutely innocent people in our Shankill community, adding, "Some wounded folks are fighting for their lives in hospitals right now!

"But," I said, touched deeply by the brutal truth, "Protestant terrorists must take some of the responsibility. I am NOT justifying what has happened, but if nine members of (Loyalist) Ulster Freedom Fighters had died in the bomb blast, instead of nine innocent civilians, the Shankill community would have accepted it more easily!"

I clarified my statement, so that no one might misinterpret my meaning in the Shankill. I articulated that our community would certainly have been angry if nine members of the UFF had been killed, but these murders of innocent men, women and children were *beyond reprehensible*!

Church on the Wall

The UDA and the UFF took great offense at the words I believe God motivated me to speak to all of Northern Ireland that day. But I had stirred up the most powerful nest of wasps in the Shankill.

Sixteen prominent UDA leaders met to decide if what I had spoken warranted a death sentence, and these 16 terrorists voted to have me shot dead. They had interpreted my words to mean that I wished that Loyalist Protestant leaders would have been blown to bits — instead of the innocent people who had died. Someone with connection to the UDA immediately warned me to leave Belfast.

I prayed for wisdom, knowing that when the UDA targeted someone in the Shankill, the newspapers soon carried his obituary. I worried about my Kathleen and the kids — Jonathan was 17, Chara was 14 and Paula was 11 — but I had no leading from the Holy Spirit to pack up and run. I made a cardinal choice — one that struck the deepest chords of faith in my consciousness.

I put my trust in Jesus, who holds all power of life and death, and kept the worries of my death sentence between God and me.

Jack McKee is not a brave man. Looking back, these events seem surreal and miraculous beyond my ken. The week of my sentence, I sauntered the length of Shankill Road once, then crossed the street and walked back down the other side.

Two young men (climbing the ladder of UDA power) volunteered to carry out my execution on the same night that I scheduled an evangelism meeting at our New Life Fellowship. The meeting usually lasted from 7:30 p.m. until 10 p.m.

Ten minutes after I left my home, my two assassins arrived at my house. Seeing that my Renault was gone, they hid at a vacant house across the street waiting for me to return.

Our meeting at the church ended at 10 p.m., like usual, and as I was about to leave, at about 10:10 p.m., my evangelism leader stopped me. "Pastor, before you go, would you mind if we prayed for you? I don't know why, but I sense danger tonight."

My spine tingled as I felt the Holy Spirit at work. No one knew about the threat that hovered over me, except me, the UDA and God.

My wonderful friends gathered around me and took turns praying for me. I arrived at my home at 10:40 p.m. — warily glancing inside all the cars along the street and peering at shadows around the houses. I drove past our house once slowly, then turned around and drove back to my driveway, satisfied.

Seconds after locking the front door with me safely inside, a knock startled Kathleen and me. It was our neighbor.

"Don't know if this means a thing, but from 7:30 until 10:30 two men puffing on cigs stood inside that vacant house and seemed to be casing your place. I saw them drive off at 10:30 sharp."

My heart beat a little faster as I realized how our

praying to God had delayed my arrival home by 10 minutes — and saved my life.

One of my assassins had committed his first murder at 15 years old. His best friend (another former UDA member who had given his life to Christ) later related how the two killers had waited three hours for me to return, but then left.

Infighting among UDA members broke out soon after this failed attempt to kill me, and the commanders refocused their violence upon one another. Our New Life Fellowship gained a strong foothold in the community, and it wasn't until 1997 that the terrorists sentenced me to death once again.

A couple in our congregation who owned a flower shop refused to pay protection money to a paramilitary group. Thugs battered their windows and beautiful flower displays with baseball bats to send a message.

My indignation grew into a public condemnation of the racketeering rampant in the Shankill. After my television interview excoriating the organized crime in the Shankill, an Ulster Volunteer Force member came to my New Life Fellowship office to inform me that I was on their hit list.

I calmly told this brigadier, "I don't want to die, but I don't fear death. I am ready to go and know *where* I am going. As for you — you will stand before God and give an account for your actions."

The man began to defend himself, but in the 15

minutes he sat across from my desk, I explained that he did not serve the same God that I did. He stomped off in an absolute rage.

I'll never know exactly why nothing came of the UVF's initial decision to kill me. But in the following years, paramilitaries were so involved in defending their own turf (now riddled with drug dealers, enforcers, gambling and thieves), I must have been the least of their worries.

In 2001, after 11 Shankill paramilitary men were killed in a Loyalist feud, we organized a walk for peace, and 500 people joined in our march the length of Shankill Road. Wives of the paramilitary husbands dared not join in, but showed their solidarity by standing along the sidewalks.

It was just after our march for peace that I felt God drop a distasteful idea into my heart.

Build a cross like Arthur Blessitt, and walk the Shankill and Falls Roads — for 40 days.

"Okay, Lord. I'm willing to carry a cross, but why 40 days? How about *three* days ..."

I finally gave in, committing to 40 days for two hours a day. In my heart of hearts, I believed that within the first three days, if I walked the Falls Road, I needed to have my last will and testament in order. No respectable IRA brigadier would sanction a Protestant marching the Falls Road.

Miraculously, I made it through the first three days bearing the cross without incident. In fact, Sinn Fein, the political wing of the IRA, stopped by to say, "As long as you are walking with that cross, you'll be okay, Jack. If you have any problems, come see us."

God's sovereign grace is a powerful force in our world.

People on the Falls Road were trotting out of pubs to ask me what John 3:16 meant (it was painted in bright white letters on the cross). Some thought it was my given name. I had a wonderful opportunity to tell them about Jesus, who loved them and died for them so that they could have peace now and live forever with him.

My son, Jonathan, and my associate pastor were walking along the sidewalk with me one day, handing out cards explaining what John 3:16 meant, when three IRA paramilitaries accosted us. The commander stuck his finger in my chest and told me what they were going to do to my son and pastor friend if they continued to walk with me — and I began to lose my cool.

Suddenly a short, thin man came out of nowhere and took control of the situation. The three men responded respectfully when he ordered them to leave us alone. God used this senior commander in the IRA to keep us from being beaten or worse. The following days, I marched alone.

On the 39th day, I felt that God was challenging me to stop at the Irish Republican Army offices on Falls Road and give them a gift. I hated the idea, but obeyed the Holy Spirit's nudging. I left my cross outside and approached the door to the IRA headquarters, my nerves on edge.

The thin man, who had rescued my son and associate pastor on the Falls Road, invited me inside. Terrorists from the same group that kidnapped and tortured Private Bobby McComb accepted my gift — given in the spirit of forgiveness and Christ's love — which was a mirror with the verse John 3:16 in Gaelic etched in the glass.

The mirror still hangs on the wall of the IRA offices. My God-sanctioned walk on the Falls Road broke ground for a new ministry to be birthed among Catholics in the years ahead.

ৡৡৡ

When men from our New Life Fellowship launched Liberty Taxis Company, Loyalist paramilitaries decided that Jack McKee and his drivers must pay dearly for cutting in on their lucrative territory.

We created Liberty Taxis in 2005 to provide employment for men in Belfast and serve the public with honest, dependable, safe service. Some of the taxi drivers, who worked for the taxi companies owned by paramilitaries, jumped ship and came to work for us.

Liberty taxis seldom waited for fares, while the paramilitary-owned taxis often sat idle.

One day a UDA commander dropped by my house, and I invited him inside. He tossed a copy of a widely read newspaper article at me and challenged me about quotes in the piece attributed to me. I had compared the paramilitaries in Belfast to organized crime.

"Look," I said, "you and I both know the truth: The taxi companies in Belfast belong to or pay protection money to paramilitaries. If you want to take issue with the newspaper, that's up to you. But everyone knows how things are here."

It was midnight when the commander left my home. I didn't expect a personal reprisal, even though our phone lines to the church had been cut and several taxis driven by our men had been firebombed.

At 3:30 a.m. the following day, my family awoke to the sounds of shattering glass and an explosion that shook our bedroom walls. Masked men used what we believe were baseball bats to break out the dual-paned windows in the front of our house. They tried to toss bottles of petrol/ paint bombs inside, but the thugs were only able to shatter the first layer of window glass, so none of the bottles made it into the rooms. One petrol bomb ignited the gasoline and interior of my car and scorched it like an overdone marshmallow.

Later that morning I went public on all local news channels and newspapers to make it clear that I would not be going anywhere, nor would I be giving up anything I was doing. Liberty Taxis would continue.

That was before the police informed me that leaders of the paramilitaries had sanctioned attacks on our taxi drivers. It was time for me to back down and place the situation in God's hands.

Two people associated with our Liberty Taxis Company committed their lives to Christ, and in time, two of the men who attacked our home sought me out to apologize.

Declare it Fearlessly

When one of the young terrorists asked for my forgiveness, I replied, "On the night that you attacked our home, we forgave you, lad. Be assured that we don't hold it against you."

Due to the potential attacks, we chose to close Liberty Taxis, but we were able to proclaim the Gospel of love and forgiveness "in season and out."

For more than 30 years, we McKees and fellow ministers have lived, worked, played, grieved, helped, argued and reasoned with our neighbors — on both sides of the Peace Wall. It has been a painfully slow, sometimes perilous process, but Jesus has formed a foundation of credibility upon which he rescues the lost every day.

అం అం అం

To profit in Belfast in any activities controlled by the ruthless paramilitary commanders, you must pay them their cut or expect merciless retribution. Paramilitary members hauled one of our young people behind our youth center and shot him in the elbows, ankles and knees — his crime was keeping money from personal drug deals.

A mentally handicapped young man once stumbled onto a scene where Protestant paramilitary members might have been implicated. Not far from our church doors this "child in a man's body" was tortured and killed by leading members in a Protestant Loyalist group.

Church on the Wall

"Do not be overcome by evil, but overcome evil with good" (Romans 12:21).

To combat the evil that seduces our Shankill youth and families, God helped us raise money to purchase real estate on Northumberland Street — a 22,000-square-foot warehouse straddling the Peace Wall. Our New Life Centre has become our Gospel plaza, with doors opening to the Protestant Shankill Road *and* to the Catholic Falls Road.

Today our community outreach programs create opportunities and employment for women and youth. From our venue we run a powerful, internationally recognized youth interventionist program known as Higher Force Challenge.

Our range of facilities has grown to include a coffee house, a 600-seat auditorium, indoor soccer stadium, daycare facility, childcare for special-needs children and afterschool programs.

The remodeled warehouse is located on the same block where I first watched a "hippie" carrying a wooden cross down Northumberland Street in 1971 — Arthur Blessitt. I was 19 years old, Arthur was 31.

Our New Life Centre is a base of operations from which we now launch home groups and evangelistic meetings on Protestant *and* Catholic sides of the Peace Wall. Some of our congregation comes from the Falls Road, and we co-located with a drinking club in a building owned by the Workers Party, the political wing of the Official Irish Republican Army.

Declare it Fearlessly

I had visited the manager of this Official IRA Social Club to discuss the possibility of renting space next to his pub, when he responded, "Jack, you know who we are. We are socialists, anti-government, anti-religion and certainly anti-church. But we like what you're doing ..."

The room he rented us accommodates 120 people — many who come are Catholics. This side of the Peace Wall, we don't refer to our meetings as "church" (it sounds too Protestant), but we invite *everyone* to fellowship and hear the simple Gospel through testimonies delivered by men and women freed from the chains of guilt and ethnic hatred.

Official IRA drinking-club patrons drift into our meetings, sipping pints of beer. We welcome them, and they often leave our worship service for refills and come back, while the Holy Spirit speaks to their hearts.

ɔɛɔɛɔɛ

My heart was broken over an 18-year-old youth who attended New Life and participated in our 12-week intervention program. He owed a local paramilitary commander money for drug deals and couldn't pay. He was ordered to appear at a certain location for punishment. Driven by fears of torture, the young man took his own life.

In 1971, not far from our present New Life Centre, the IRA threatened to nail Arthur Blessitt to the cross he carried; 40 years later, Arthur answered my invitation to come to Northern Ireland again. Arthur was 71, and I was 59 when we carried crosses together on the Shankill and Falls Roads — to shine a light on a new epidemic sweeping Belfast: suicide.

Despair can be as deadly as any bullet. Nearly 300 people take their lives in Northern Ireland each year, and death by suicide has seen a 100 percent increase in just 15 years, according to BBC News Northern Ireland.

Hundreds of people walked with Arthur and me as we demonstrated that the message of God's love in Northern Ireland will never be silenced — not by paramilitaries or Satan himself.

Rain or shine, inside our "Church on the Wall," Protestants and Catholics gather to play games, to root for soccer teams, to exercise and study, eat or sip teas and coffees. Each week young people rock to Jesus-centered bands and hobnob in youth groups. On this neutral ground, youth and adults experience God's love among seasoned believers who know their purpose for living — and share their lives. Our dream of becoming a safe "street corner" for all faiths, ethnic groups and political persuasions is coming true.

Together we pray for the day when Jesus deluges Northern Ireland with "the peace of God, which transcends all understanding."

The Great Amazon Adventure
The Story of David Pepper
Written by Karen Koczwara

God, I pray thee, light these idle sticks of my life, and may I burn for thee. Consume my life, my God, for it is thine. I seek not a long life, but a full one, like you, Lord Jesus.

These powerful words were scrawled into the journal of a charismatic young man named Jim Elliot. Just 21 years old, Elliot had completely devoted his life to God as a missionary. Little did he know that the desire of his heart would be fulfilled just a few years later when his life abruptly and tragically ended.

After ministering to the Quechua Indians in Ecuador, Elliot learned about the Huaorani, a small, particularly violent jungle tribe. Elliot and four other missionary friends attempted to make friendly contact with the Huaorani, dropping clothing and various trinkets from an airplane above the tribe's village. Elliot learned several simple Huaorani phrases and tried to communicate with the people. The tribe initially seemed receptive to their gestures, even sending gifts back in return. At last, Elliot and his missionary friends deemed the area safe enough to land, and they set up camp at a sandbar they dubbed Palm Beach.

Declare it Fearlessly

On January 8, 1956, Elliot and his friends went to greet the Huaorani at Palm Beach but were blindsided by a violent attack. All five men were speared to death by this tribe they had come to trust. Their bodies were found in the river by a search and rescue team several days later. On January 14, the men were buried in a common grave on Palm Beach in the midst of a tropical storm.

The story immediately made international headlines. *Life* magazine covered the deaths of the five brave men with a poignant photo essay, and missionary organizations all over the world took notice. Elliot and his friends soon gained martyr status for their attempt to spread the Gospel message to this dangerous tribe. Elliot's wife, Elisabeth, would go on to return to the jungles of Ecuador to minister to the very people who had brutally killed her husband.

Jim Elliot's words, "He is no fool who gives what he cannot keep to gain that which he cannot lose," would become one of the most influential phrases in all of evangelical history. His story impacted not just missionaries, but many others as well. One was a 14-year-old boy from Philadelphia. Deeply moved after hearing the news of Jim Elliot's death, the teenager felt compelled to spend time alone with God. He then boldly prayed, "God, I will go to the jungles of South America."

That boy was my father.

స~స~స

The Great Amazon Adventure

After high school, my father attended Bible college, then headed out to start his missions work along the Amazon River of Peru. Upon arriving in the capital city of Lima, he met a woman named Carlene, and six months after an expedition into the jungle, he proposed. In February 1964, he and Carlene flew back to the United States to marry, landing first in Atlanta. My father bought a hamburger and a milkshake, and then they flew on to Philadelphia, where his parents met them at the airport. His mother asked him how much money he had. He reached into his pockets, pulled out a dime, a nickel and three pennies and handed her the coins. His father then pulled him aside.

"How much money do you have, son?" his father asked.

"Well, I had 18 cents, but Mom already took the coins, so now I'm broke," he replied.

"How are you going to support your new wife?" his father pressed, staring at the measly coins.

"I'm going to be a faith missionary," my father said heartily.

My father married Carlene, and the two, both feeling strongly called to the jungles of Peru, settled there, near the Tapiche River. My father's mother took the coins and placed them in a picture frame, along with a handwritten note. The "18 Cents Story" would live on as a reminder that when one is called to do God's work as a missionary, he must go in faith, no matter how much or how little he has.

Declare it Fearlessly

The jungles of Peru boasted a variety of beautiful, tropical plants, trees and creatures. Tall, lush foliage lined the stunning Amazon River, postcard-perfect in all its glory. But a pervading darkness lingered beyond the vibrant colors. The villagers of Peru needed the light of Jesus and the hope that came only from him.

From the time he arrived, my father held a burden for reaching the Matses Indians, an indigenous tribe of the Peruvian and Brazilian Amazon. Also known as the Mayoruna, their name originated from the Quechua language and meant "river people." These Indians relied heavily on the plant and animal life of the surrounding rainforest and were especially adept at hunting with bows and arrows. They were also quite violent, often fighting with the local military and causing trouble. Wearing no clothes, they tore through villages and raided them, snatching women and young girls, killing men and stealing items. Sometimes, they completely plundered entire villages to the ground.

Desperate to reach these uncivilized people, my father built a river house near the Matses, hoping to establish a relationship with them. It was a bold move, one he knew could cost him his life. The Matses were dangerous and unpredictable — a threatening force. But though they boasted strong survival techniques, they lacked the one thing my father believed they needed — a relationship with Jesus Christ.

Despite his best efforts, my father was not able to make contact with the notorious Matses people. He and my mother moved on, traveling up and down the local rivers and trying to establish relationships with other villagers. After arriving in the village of San Vincente on the Tapichi River, a local witch doctor approached my father with a harsh warning.

"You will experience suffering and pain," the witch doctor told them angrily, cursing my father for his attempts to reach the people.

My father knew the task ahead of him was not an easy one. A Catholic church just up the river had been shut down, as the people were very resistant to anything outside their tribal beliefs. But he also knew that, with God's help, anything was possible. He remembered the story of Jim Elliot, the brave young man who had persisted in reaching out to the Huaorani people of Ecuador. God had called my father to the jungle, and he would be faithful to help my father complete his mission.

For the next year and a half, my parents continued going back to the village of San Vincente. They learned that the witch doctor had tried to burn down the home of the pastor in the village. But a neighbor witnessed the act, and after he reported it, the witch doctor lost all credibility and power and was promptly kicked out of the village. This paved the way for the Gospel message, and the local people became open to hearing God's word from that moment on. Their hearts softened, and God began to do a miraculous work in their midst.

My father traveled from village to village, evangelizing to the tribal people. Despite a lack of training in the medical field, he performed dental work for those in need, sometimes pulling up to 70 rotten teeth in one day. He also offered basic aid and even delivered a few babies. While the adults were more reluctant to accept his gestures, the teenagers and children remained especially receptive. He began a Vacation Bible School in San Vincente, speeding up and down the rivers in his boat every day to pick up children from four other villages for the special event.

One day, my father stopped at the village of Yurina to drop off the children. There, six men approached him, all carrying machetes.

"Don't get off the boat, or we'll kill you!" a short, burly man barked. "You are not welcome here!"

Fear-based rumors had begun circulating years before, stating that all white missionaries wanted to kill kids and make products out of their body parts. The villagers had been suspicious of white people ever since. My father knew he would have to act carefully in order to prove his upright intentions.

My father picked up a little New Testament Bible and waved it in the air. "I have this Gospel for your village," he said. "Which of you is machismo enough to read it?"

The short, burly man stepped forward. "I will take it," he said, meeting my father's eyes.

The man introduced himself as Adino Valentine Ruiz. As my father handed him the Bible, he noticed bloody lesions on the man's hands and feet. This man was a leper, suffering from a terrible, debilitating condition. Just moments before, he'd threatened to kill my father, and now, his heart had been softened. God was indeed doing a good work in the jungles of Peru.

My parents continued to minister to the local villagers, and the teenagers, children and women were receptive. But the men remained more difficult to reach. One day, my father encountered a man named Mauricio in the village of Manicamire, located on the Nanay River. A short, handsome man with a strong build, Mauricio was also a drunk who hated Christians. After observing my parents interacting with the other villagers, Mauricio finally approached them. My father handed him a New Testament Bible and addressed him with confidence. "One day, you will be the leader of a church."

When my parents returned to Mauricio's village several months later, they discovered a completely new man who had given up drinking in exchange for following God. "I prayed and asked God to change me," Mauricio said with a smile. "I am now leading a church, just as you said I would."

My father praised God for the wonderful work he'd done in Mauricio's life. Mauricio now held church services in the local school building, as well as in homes. Though he had no formal pastoral training, Mauricio used God's word as a guide to reach the local people. My parents began attending services at Mauricio's church in Manicamire, and as the weeks went by, they began to see God work miracles not just in people's hearts, but on their bodies as well.

Declare it Fearlessly

One night, the villagers rushed to my parents with some devastating news. "There is a terrible epidemic, and people are dying here!" they cried.

My father went to the church and began preaching, praying and laying hands on sickly people. He came from a charismatic background, and my mother had been raised in a Pentecostal church. They both strongly believed in the healing power of prayer and knew that miracles were not just reserved for Biblical times, but still took place today. For two nights straight, they laid hands on people and prayed. In the process, amazing occurrences began to take place. A deaf child's hearing was completely restored, and those with terrible fevers, who'd seemed mere hours away from death's door, were completely healed. As a teen, my father had attended many healing revivals with evangelists like A.A. Allen, Jack Coe and William Branham in Philadelphia. He had witnessed many miracles, but in all his years of praying for the sick, this was the first time he'd seen every single person who came forward be healed. Again, he praised God, giving him all the glory.

I was born on June 1, 1967, two years after my sister. One day, when I was 3 years old, I played outside on my tricycle near the Amazon River in Iquitos where we lived. Suddenly, my 5-year-old sister began to shriek in terror.

"Daddy, there is a snake by David!" she cried. She pointed to a striped 5-foot cascavel rattlesnake slithering on the patio two feet from my little bike.

My father's friend, visiting from America, ran for his gun. Meanwhile, my father raced over and began

The Great Amazon Adventure

stomping on the snake, doing everything he could to kill it before it sprung and attacked me. When the snake was dead, everyone breathed a sigh of relief. As I grew older, I would come to realize just how dangerous this venomous pit viper truly was. Its venom had the potential to paralyze and even kill a human being. God was truly watching out for my family in this often-perilous jungle land.

While my parents made their initial home on a houseboat, they eventually settled into a home on land after a barge hit their boat and it sank. Every year, the Amazon River flooded, and the waters rushed up to our house and sometimes even seeped inside the walls. We took advantage of the opportunity, catching the fish that swam right onto our patio. I enjoyed my own bedroom, and when my younger sister arrived four years after me, we moved into a house in the heart of Iquitos. There, she and my older sister shared a bedroom. We did not have a TV and received all form of news communication through radio. Because we had no access to electronics, we spent our free time playing marbles, swimming in the rivers, flying kites and "playing church." Creativity was a necessity.

My sisters and I attended an English-speaking school with a few other missionary kids. Two maids attended to the duties at home, as my parents spent most of their day out on the mission field. The maids walked us to school and prepared us breakfast and lunch. When my parents returned in the evening, we all ate dinner together, then played a few games before bed. Monkey, turtle, anteater and alligator were among the more unusual foods we dined on. Though our conditions were primitive, we always had plenty, and I learned from a young age to trust in God for all our needs.

Heat seemed to permeate the jungle year round, cloaking us in its stickiness. When the rain fell, the air cooled a bit, but it quickly warmed up again. Certain parts of the jungle boasted 100-degree weather and 100 percent humidity. Our clothes clung to our backs, sweat trickled down our brow and our heads felt like they might explode as we treaded through the day. The jungle people rose at 4 a.m., completing their most burdensome tasks before the sun rose. They then ate a light meal and took a siesta at noon, sleeping for several hours while the sun beat down outside. When darkness fell, they went to bed, then repeated the cycle all over the next morning. Some homes used electricity, but many relied on generators, which ran during certain hours of the day. Life was both simple and challenging, but I did not know any other way.

My family settled in Iquitos, the largest city in the Peruvian rainforest and the fifth-largest city in Peru. Nestled at the Amazon Basin along the Amazon, Nanay and Itaya Rivers, it boasted four districts with a total population of roughly 400,000 people. The city was originally developed by Jesuit missionaries along the Nanay River in the mid-1700s and rose to temporary wealth and development during the 20th century rubber industry boom. Only accessible by airplane or boat, it remained the largest city in the world inaccessible by road.

The Great Amazon Adventure

Most people in the city traveled on buses, motorcycles or *motokars*. Traditional vehicles were sparse. Many people traveled by foot around downtown Iquitos, which featured the Belen Market, the largest traditional market in the Peruvian Amazon. Supermarkets did not exist, and canned goods were rare. While those with a higher education pursued jobs as store managers, nurses, doctors or pilots, farmers and fishermen made up a large portion of the working population in the villages. Tourism remained a large portion of the industry in the area, and many laborers sold their goods at the marketplace. Locals flocked to the outdoor markets every Saturday to purchase fresh foods for the week. I soon became accustomed to the strong smell of fish that permeated the air.

When I was 6 years old, I began evangelizing in the marketplace with my father. He situated my sister on one side of the street, and I stood on the other, passing out tracts to everyone who walked by. If anyone had questions about God, church or any other spiritual matters, I directed them to my father nearby. I loved working alongside my father as he shared the Gospel and looked forward to these times each week. God was stirring in my own heart, and I strongly sensed his presence with me wherever I went. I wanted to know more about him.

At age 7, I prayed at a church meeting, inviting Jesus into my life. Though just a young boy, I had seen my father live out a life of faith, always persevering in the midst of trials. He inspired me with his attitude of trust, joy and peace, and I wanted to be more like him. But my invitation for salvation was just the beginning of my journey, as God would have much more in store for me down the road.

One morning, my father awoke to discover that all four tires on his 1969 Chevelle had been slashed. My father had been forced to confront someone who'd tried to steal money from his organization, and he suspected they might have been responsible for the malicious act. He left later that morning in another vehicle to take his two friends to the airport, and when they arrived, they were still discussing the frustrating situation.

"All four tires, slashed! I can't believe it," my father said, shaking his head. "It must have been someone who is disgruntled."

A man standing nearby overheard the conversation, walked up to my father and handed him a wad of cash. As the man sauntered away, my father stared after him in awe, then began to count the money. To his amazement, the cash totaled even more than the amount needed for new tires, as well as enough to make other repairs on the car.

"God is so good!" he exclaimed, deeply touched by the stranger's generosity. "I needed new tires, anyway. Those ones were nearly bald," my father said, chuckling as he carefully pocketed the money.

I loved watching my father in action, seeing him live out his faith in a radical way. Whether preaching the Gospel in the marketplace or sharing from God's word at a church service, he never wavered in the midst of opposition. He often preached a sermon about perseverance, using the phrase, "Plod on, plod on, plod on," to encourage people to stick to what God had called them to in the midst of trials. From an early age, I learned that a life of ministry was not always easy, but it was always worth sticking out.

When not evangelizing or spending time with our family, my father busied himself with various construction projects along the river, helping to build and remodel structures in the villages. Always a vivacious and curious boy, I loved working alongside him, helping mix concrete or carry supplies. Often, I became more of a nuisance than a help, but our time together provided some of my fondest memories.

A preacher named Wayne Meyer came to Iquitos to speak at the Bible Academy. My parents often attended services and classes there, while I played outside with the other children.

One night when I was 8, my mother raced out, grabbed me and pulled me into the room where the service was in session. The moment I walked in, I realized something indescribable was taking place inside those walls. Wayne Meyer laid hands on me and began praying. To my amazement, I began speaking in a language I did not know. I had been filled with the Holy Spirit for the very first time. Later, I would understand just how powerful that moment was. It was as if the Holy Spirit had descended like a cloud onto the entire room, and the presence of God was strong in our midst. After praying, I scampered back outside to play, but the experience lingered in my mind for years.

As I watched my father fall in love with the people of Peru, I began to fall in love with them, too. Having been raised since birth in the jungle, I knew no other way of life. Though my skin color differed from theirs, I soon realized we weren't very different after all. They enjoyed a strong sense of family and cared for those in need. If a child became orphaned, another family member quickly took that child in and raised it as his or her own. They also loved to dance and sing as they worshipped God, swaying back and forth in their colorful garb. Though most had little, their faces radiated undeniable joy and gratitude. Many were receptive to my father's ministry and put their faith in God. My father performed numerous water baptisms, encouraging the people to declare their faith publically. But he had to proceed with caution, as deadly piranhas swam in certain parts of the rivers where the people wished to be baptized. Life in the jungle, I learned, never held a dull moment.

One day, a visitor navigated the path from the river to our home. The man was Adino Valentine Ruiz, the leper who years before had taken the New Testament Bible from my father just minutes after threatening his life. After reading the Bible my father gave him, he put his faith in Christ and started a home church in Yurina. He went for training at the Bible Academy and became an evangelist on the rivers.

"I am a preacher now!" Adino told my father excitedly.

The Great Amazon Adventure

"After reading your Bible, I was drawn to God's word, and I began gathering people and preaching to them!"

Adino's physical condition had worsened, and his fingers were now missing. He gave my father a big hug. As my father embraced this crippled man, he knew it would be a powerful moment he'd cherish forever.

As they pulled apart, my mother cried, "Bill, you're bleeding!"

Bloody prints stood out on his shirt. She soon realized the blood came from Adino's lesions, not from my father's skin.

My father's heart surged with joy. God was using a once-hardened leper to reach people with the Gospel! He kept in contact with Adino and was amazed by the man's passion for God. When I met him, I looked into his eyes and was completely transfixed by the love of God I saw in them. Despite his bloody, deteriorating condition, joy danced on Adino's face and radiated all around him. Adino was a walking miracle.

Adino paddled up and down the Tapichi River, sharing the Gospel with everyone he could. When it became too difficult for him to paddle his small boat, the villagers purchased a motorboat for him, which provided more efficient transportation. Adino proclaimed that when he died, he wanted to pass from this life into eternity while preaching. One day, after sharing an especially moving sermon, Adino returned home, where he passed away later that afternoon. The leper with a heart for God had nearly gotten his wish.

Declare it Fearlessly

When I turned 9, my parents decided that their assignment in the jungle was done. They had witnessed many miracles during their years there and seen God transform the lives of some of the most hardened men and women. They had seen many churches erected, and even the local Bible Academy began to thrive. Like Jim Elliot, my father had forged boldly into places no one else had dared touch. Despite the primitive and often dangerous conditions, his deep faith in God had not wavered in even the most perilous times. The 14-year-old boy who had once eagerly said, "I'll go to the jungle," had done just that, and because of his step of faith, many had come to Christ. I had watched my father carefully, hoping to emulate the same faith he expressed. God was already stirring my own heart, prompting me to follow him. I did not know what our future entailed, but I was certain God did.

Though my father was not able to reach the Matses Indians during his time in Peru, two other missionaries found success. Harriet Fields and Hattie Kneeland, both Wycliffe Bible Translators, decided to march deep into the Amazon, armed with Tupperware, flowered tablecloths and seven spoken languages between them. Two ordinary women from Indiana and Missouri, they were keenly aware of the Matses' dangerous ways. Harriet, a former insurance office secretary who grew up on a farm, was prepared to fully put her faith to the test by reaching this otherwise unreachable tribe. Hattie, a bit more timid, expressed initial reluctance to leave her comfort zone, but God nudged her heart as well.

The Great Amazon Adventure

The women boldly marched into the jungle and established peaceful, sustained contact with the Matses tribe. They developed a genuine friendship with the unruly people and soon earned their trust. While sharing the Gospel with them, they also introduced them to practical ways of civilization, including wearing clothes. Up until then, the Matses had run around fully naked. The women helped them plant trees and taught them other basic life skills. Miraculously, the Matses began giving their lives over to God.

Our family moved to Willow, Alaska, where my father prayerfully decided to pursue global leadership and pastoral training. Though he was now half a world away from the jungles of Peru, his story with the Matses Indians was not over yet. In fact, it was just beginning.

ɁɁɁ

At 9 years old, I decided to undergo water baptism at our church in Anchorage, Alaska. We had only been in the United States a few months, still acclimating to life outside the jungle. After witnessing so many miraculous baptisms in the piranha-ridden jungle rivers, I wanted to boldly declare my faith before all my family and new friends. As the pastor held me under the water for what seemed like an especially long time, I wondered when he'd lift me up. *Good thing I did a lot of swimming in the Amazon and can hold my breath for a long time,* I thought to myself, trying to keep calm.

Declare it Fearlessly

As the pastor lifted me out of the water, I felt the Holy Spirit speak distinctly to me.

You are called to preach the Gospel.

Wow, God, really? Okay!

I climbed out of the water, and the pastor asked me to share my testimony with the crowd. I stepped forward and spoke. "I know that God has called me to preach the Gospel," I said confidently. And from that moment on, I knew that I would. I was not sure if I would return to the jungles of Peru or pastor a local church someday, but I was certain God would make his plan clear in his time.

While I loved God with all my heart, I struggled throughout my next few years. Moving to the United States proved a bit of a culture shock. I was used to being the blue-eyed, blond-haired kid who stood out in a crowd. I'd always felt unique, special even. In Alaska, I was just another kid in a sea of other kids. I also sensed a more lackadaisical atmosphere at the churches we attended. Living in the jungle, I'd seen and experienced radical things, from physical miracles to spiritual miracles as well. The Peruvian people boasted an uncontainable joy and excitement about life, despite their often-challenging circumstances. I'd seen my father trust God in lean and good times and learned to trust God, too. I wanted to live an extraordinary life, but would I ever find my place in the United States?

At age 15, I began rebelling, drinking and partying with friends. Downing a few beers seemed like the best way to fit in, so I went along with the crowd. But I never

The Great Amazon Adventure

forgot the clear message God had given me at my baptism: *You are called to preach the Gospel.* I knew this was my destiny, and after a couple years of late-night partying and morning-after hangovers, I gave up the rebellious lifestyle.

In 1985, at just 17 years old, I graduated early from high school. That spring and summer, I took up commercial fishing. While many of my friends went on to obtain a traditional college degree, I knew that wasn't my path. I wanted to focus on seeking God and solidifying my relationship with him. That fall, I began studies at Pinecrest Bible Training Center in Salisbury Center, New York.

In 1988, I met a beautiful girl named LaRae. My sister set us up on a blind date, and from the moment we connected, I knew she was special. At 5 feet, 6 inches, with brown hair and green eyes, she was lovely on the outside, but it was her heart I was especially attracted to.

"I want to serve the Lord with my life," LaRae told me, her eyes sparkling.

After just four dates, I asked her to marry me. I was completely confident she was the one God had chosen for me. She happily accepted, and on September 24, 1988, we married.

We welcomed our first child, LaRiesa, into the world on October 29, 1990. Another daughter, Jessica, followed in 1993. And in 1995, we welcomed twins Colton and Emily into the world. That same year, I bought my first commercial fishing boat and permit to fish in Prince William Sound. Life moved along at a steady, comfortable pace, but I knew commercial fishing was not my final stop. God had more in store for my life.

In 1997, I felt God speak to me, strongly urging me to pursue ministry. Like an unquenchable fire in my chest, the call to ministry grew stronger every day. *It's time, David. You have to do it. It's time to proclaim what God has given you.*

I obeyed God and became a youth pastor and associate pastor at Maranatha Fellowship in Anchorage, Alaska, for the next three years. I continued commercial fishing as a way to provide for my growing family. Our lives were busy and full, but they were about to take yet another turn.

In February 2000, I felt God prompting me to begin a church. LaRae and I started a home church in Wasilla, beginning by meeting with just a handful of families in a living room. The group continued to grow and grow, and before long, we realized we needed an official church building. We called ourselves Church on the Rock. Little did I know God's plans for our church were bigger than I could imagine.

That same year, I traveled back to Peru for the second time since leaving the country at 9 years old. Much of the country still looked the same, but much had changed as well. More vehicles lined the roads, and many people now had access to modern technology. But witch doctors still practiced in some areas, and idolatry remained a troubling problem. God began to stir my heart again as I explored the very jungles I'd traipsed through as a child. I knew that God had called me to preach the Gospel, and I knew that he wanted me in ministry. Church on the Rock was just sprouting from its roots and starting to grow. But would God keep me in Alaska, or would I return to the land I'd imprinted my first footsteps on?

In 2001, my father returned to Peru, along with a team of South African pastors. The head chief of the Matses, Ildebrando, along with his tribal leaders, welcomed my father's group. "We want your help," Ildebrando said boldly. "We want Bibles. We want our pastors to be trained. We want metal roofs for our churches. We want someone to live with us and show us the way."

"Perfect," my father replied enthusiastically.

The head chief met with my father and the other pastors at a local hotel and discussed his needs in depth. Ildebrando, slightly taller than the average Matses man at 5 feet, 5 inches, possessed a gentle but confident air. As my father talked with him, he thanked God for the miraculous changes in the Matses tribe. As a newlywed with a passion for the people of the jungle, he had specifically prayed to reach these once-uncivilized people. Though he had not been able to make contact with them, God had used two ordinary but brave women to deliver the Gospel message. The people who once threatened and violently killed outsiders now welcomed them onto their land. They planted crops and trees, sent their children to school and dressed in Western wear. But most importantly, many of them loved Jesus. They had something more powerful than bows and arrows — they had the Gospel. My father's prayers had been answered.

Declare it Fearlessly

In 2002, I sold my fishing boat and gave up my permit, trading a life of commercial fishing for fulltime ministry. I continued to pastor Church on the Rock in Alaska, and it grew exponentially each year. While I loved preaching and thanked God for my ministry, a large piece of my heart always remained with the people of the jungle.

In 2004, I returned to Peru again and visited some of the most un-contacted tribes in the land. My team and I had sent ahead supplies to dedicate a local church, and we planned to conduct a conference there. The area we'd be traveling to was so remote that it was only accessible by boat. As we prepared to leave for our mission, we learned that the river's water levels were dropping so significantly that we wouldn't be able to get up to the church.

"We will go as far as we can," I told my team. "And we will pray."

My team and I prayed, asking God to provide a way for us to reach the church. We then went to bed. In the morning, we discovered that the water levels had risen an astounding two feet.

"Amazing!" we cried, praising God for this miracle.

"I didn't think you would come," the head chief said when we arrived, staring at us in disbelief. "Thank God you are here."

I traveled back to Peru several times over the next few years, always eager to meet new people, share God's love and spread the word of God to those who had still never heard of Jesus Christ. It was exciting to see church buildings and Bible academies sprout up in areas that had once been untouched by the Gospel. The people were receptive and hungry, ready to receive and give back in return.

While visiting one of the Matses' churches one day, I became perplexed at their style of worship. They clapped while singing, but at first, it sounded to me like the worst rhythm I'd ever heard in all my travels around the world. *I'm not sure there are any two people who are actually clapping in synch in the entire church,* I thought. But as I watched their sincere, joyful faces, I suddenly realized that their clapping resembled the sound of the Amazon rain when it fell to the ground. *Wow, they are worshipping God in their own unique way. This is really an amazing experience to be a part of,* I concluded, deeply moved.

I became close with the Matses people and enjoyed seeing God work in their lives. In one particular church meeting, a man stood up to share his testimony and held up a picture.

"I was once a naked Mayoruna," the man said, waving the picture of his former self in the air.

Praise you, God! I stared in awe at the man who'd once run wild in the jungle, ready to kill anyone who threatened his way of life. By the power of Jesus, he was now completely changed from the inside out and living for Christ. *What a testimony! And he is just one of many, God!*

Back in Alaska, Church on the Rock soon grew to 2,000 people. The little church that had begun in a humble living room now included four different locations. I loved my ministry there but sensed God leading me on. My trips to Peru reminded me that despite how far we'd come in reaching the local people, we still had a long way to go. Many children only attended primary school, and few pursued higher education. Sickness still prevailed, and access to medicine remained limited and primitive. A cholera epidemic threatened whole areas. Chickens wandered through houses, spreading disease. Alcoholism remained a pressing problem, and drug use ran rampant in certain places as well. I also learned that Peru was the leading producer of cocaine. *God, these people need the Gospel, but they also need tangible help. We must be a light to them spiritually and physically, too.*

In 2008, I took my youngest three children on a month-long global missions trip to Egypt, Sri Lanka and India. For the first time, my children witnessed the Gospel being delivered amidst strong persecution. Buddhism, Islam and Hinduism dominated these countries, and many locals were not receptive to our efforts to share God's word. My heart broke for the many people who did not know Jesus. But I also praised God for the opportunity to share the experience with my children. God had stirred my heart toward missions after seeing my father in action, and I knew he might stir my children's hearts as well.

In December 2012, I returned to Peru and met with the Directiva of the Mission Evangelical Pentecostal Independent (MEPI). The Peruvians had chosen this name for their church network, and I was thrilled to see how it had grown. During my visit, I preached in churches, taught pastors and spent time ministering to children. As I looked into the eyes of these people I'd grown to know and love, my heart surged with joy. From the time I was a young boy, watching my father preach to the people in the marketplace, I'd understood that relationships were the most important thing in life. A relationship with God was key, but relationships with others were vitally important as well. Whether meeting in a large church, a living room, a soccer field or a school facility, I'd seen God work in mighty ways. It was exciting to see the Peruvian people adopt the same vision I had for spreading the Gospel. They, too, wanted to make disciples and replicate the work my father had started there so many years before.

"We want you to do the work your father has done here," the Peruvian people told me, excitement dancing in their eyes.

I recalled with fondness the many times I'd sat at my father's side, listening to him preach without fear. I remembered his many stories of faith, how he'd praised God when a stranger at the airport paid for his new tires, when he'd said yes to God and became a missionary, despite having only 18 cents in his pocket. My father had loved the Peruvian people with God's love, and even when times seemed treacherous and impossible, he'd never stopped trusting in his Savior. It was time for me to carry the torch, just as my father had after learning of Jim Elliot's brave mission to the Huaorani people. It was time for me to return to the jungles of Peru, this time for good.

Declare it Fearlessly

❧❧❧

The chilly air whipped at my cheeks as I sped through the snow, the white powder flying in all directions around me. It was another brisk Alaskan winter day, and I was out for a ride on my snowmobile. As I glanced ahead at the blanket of snow, then up at the vast blue sky, I thanked God for his beautiful creation. Living in Alaska for more than 30 years, I'd had access to nearly every outdoor sport and activity imaginable — running, hiking, rafting, fishing, hunting, snowmobiling and ATV riding.

I'm going to miss this, I thought wistfully. *It's been quite an adventure here. But another one is about to begin.*

With Church on the Rock now thriving, I know it is officially time for me to move on. My children are now all nearly grown. LaRiesa, 23, is training to be a paramedic. Jessica, 20, is earning a nursing degree and talks of pursuing missions in Sudan after completing an internship in Uganda. The twins, now 18, lead busy lives as well. Colton graduated high school early and looks forward to taking up commercial fishing as I once did. Emily plans to work with Youth With a Mission, an international ministry, after graduation. All of them strongly love the Lord and want to serve him with their lives, and nothing gives me and my wife greater joy.

My parents, now in their 70s, still reside in Wasilla, Alaska. My father travels globally for leadership conferences and loves to visit closed nations where Christians are still persecuted heavily. He visits Peru often, and his heart remains with the wonderful people there. While many his age live a leisurely life of retirement, my father prefers adventure, always willing to go where God leads him.

I am currently transitioning to become the President of Amazon Outreach and look forward to spending more of my time in the jungle. I plan to travel around the country there, connecting with and supporting current churches and helping to plant more. Raising up new leaders remains one of my strongest passions. I love seeing people say yes to God and give up their lives to serve him, then turn and teach others to do the same.

Jim Elliot, the brave missionary who inspired my father, once wrote in his journal, "Oh, the fullness, pleasure, sheer excitement of knowing God on earth!" Though I did not know Jim Elliot, I share in his sentiments. I know that I have been called to minister to the people of the jungle, as they have become near and dear to my heart. I want to live like Jim Elliot, enjoying each day to the fullest, serving God in any way I can.

One of my favorite life verses, Acts 20:24, reads, "However, I consider my life worth nothing to me; my only aim is to finish the race and complete the task the Lord Jesus has given me — the task of testifying to the good news of God's grace."

I watched my father live out this verse as he ministered to the people of Peru when I was a child. And from an early age, I yearned to follow in his footsteps. Now my journey has come full circle as I return to the place I once called home.

I cannot wait for the next adventure to begin.

Part I: Moving Mountains
The Story of Dominic Russo
Written by Alexine Garcia

Hopelessness hung heavy in the air, like a permanent raincloud drawn over India. I had never experienced such dark depression as I did that day watching hundreds of people bathe in the murky water of the Ganges River. Far to the right, people burned the dead and spread the ashes through the water. People washed dirty laundry on my left. And right in front of me a tall Indian man emerged from the river. Beads of water dripped down his weathered skin, his wavy silver hair and long beard. A long stripe of red blood lay smeared across his forehead, probably from a visit to the temple earlier that day. He drank the water and splashed his body.

I climbed down the steps and walked straight up to him. I spoke to him through a translator, "Why are you drinking this water? Don't you see the filth? Ashes and disease are floating in the river!"

The man pointed violently to his chest with his index finger. "I am trying to be made clean."

I gazed at him with compassion. "This river cannot wash you clean. Only the river that flows from the cross of Jesus Christ can make you clean." I continued to explain who Jesus was for the next 30 minutes, and I watched this man's heart unfold. As he gave his life over to Christ, I saw the verses in John, chapter 4, play out before me. A profound truth was revealed in that moment. There were more people in these dark recesses of life waiting for an instant change than lived across the street from my own home. Here in the world the field really was "white for the harvest."

☙☙☙

I was not your average pastor's kid. I liked church. Dennis Tinerino, a former Mr. Universe and competitive body builder, was the special guest speaker at my dad's church the particular evening that my whole life changed. He had won Mr. Universe four times, along with many other titles. The high school gym buzzed with a low rumble of people waiting for the service to start.

He gave his testimony of a life filled with drugs, alcohol, women and then time in prison. After he got out of prison, he gave his life to Christ and went on to share the Gospel around the United States. As he spoke about the need for salvation in the world, my heart raced.

"Some of you have a special call on your life. If that is you, you need to come down to the altar now."

I sat surrounded by a group of my friends. At only 12 years of age, I felt God calling me to leave my friends behind in their seats and kneel at the altar. My obedience to God was rewarded with a special experience of God's presence. I fell to the floor of that gym as God placed a vision behind my closed eyes. I began to envision a crowd of people as far and as wide as I could see. As I looked closer, I saw individual faces. There were all colors of skin. Every ethnicity imaginable was gathered together in this crowd. As I looked out, amazed at these people, a physical pain clenched my heart. The emotion was too much to bear, and I began to weep. I realized that I felt God's heartache for the nations. This was his deep compassion for those who had no relationship with him. Right in that moment, what is described in Acts 2:17 happened to me. God poured his Holy Spirit upon me.

A spiritual hunger to go out and share the Gospel with all those people in that crowd took over my life. For the next six years, I signed up for a mission trip every summer. Guatemala was the first place to capture my heart. Among the tropical green vistas and colorful buildings nestled a profound poverty. Homeless people, even children, roamed the streets and sifted through garbage. Even more evident was the lack of the Gospel in this land. As a 13-year-old boy, having lived in the United States all my life, I did not know that this kind of need even existed. My scope of reality opened up that day.

We walked the streets talking to anyone who would listen. As we spoke about Jesus, a young teenager walked right up to us and started asking questions. He wanted what Jesus had to offer. God showed me that there existed openness to spiritual things. People all over the world were ready to experience an instant change. It was such a thrill to feel God's power working through me as I spoke to this boy. This humbling experience only deepened my hunger for missions.

Declare it Fearlessly

The next summer I left for Calcutta, India, which was the poorest city in the world at that time. I thought that I had seen poverty in Guatemala, but the extent of suffering in this city was earth shattering.

While walking the streets, we passed dumpsters and trash fields where people made their homes. At night, thousands of orphaned kids covered their tiny bodies with newspaper sheets and went to sleep. Their ashy hair stuck out one end of the dirty newsprint, and their blackened feet stuck out the other.

The worship of more than 300 million Hindu gods overshadowed this place. Calcutta was named after the Hindu goddess of death and destruction, Kali, and learning this only added to the immense depression I felt there.

After a week of witnessing to the people on the streets, we left for Varanasi. The Ganges River ran through the middle of this city, the waters considered sacred by the Indian people. As we descended the steps to visit the riverside, I could not understand what people saw as holy. A putrid smell drifted off the black water. People bathed and drank the dark water. Some dipped themselves and immersed their bodies repeatedly. Others burned dead bodies right there on the banks and spread the ashes in the river. They believed that burning the people of the Brahman in the highest castes guaranteed a better place in the next life.

I will never forget that old Indian man who emerged from the water desperate to be made clean. Watching his life transform right in front of me fueled my hunger to touch the world one person at a time.

Returning home to Michigan was almost as jarring as traveling to a foreign country. In the comfort of my home, I began to question my life. I cried out to God, *I know you allowed me to see the things I witnessed. But how do I live with the same values and priorities as everyone else after what I have seen, God? How do I just act like there are not one billion people like that Indian man waiting to be changed?* From this point on, my passion became a burden, and I carried a heavy heart with me through the next several years.

Over the next few summers as a teenager, I went to Africa, South Africa and Costa Rica. I attended Oral Roberts University and led my first mission trip with a team of short-term missionaries. My friend Daniel King and I coordinated every detail and committed to bringing along 12 people. Slowly but surely, I believed, God would provide. I raised $12,500, and the rest of the team raised the funds they needed to participate. Waiting for money and resources to trickle in was like watching an icicle form.

As I stood in front of a crowd of more than 20,000 people on our first night in Puerto Plata, the largest coastal city in the Dominican Republic, the atmosphere felt electric. I gazed out on a crowd and saw with my eyes what I had only felt in my heart that day as a 12-year-old boy. We were not given a stadium, but held our event in an empty field full of trash.

Declare it Fearlessly

"The Kingdom of God has come to Puerto Plata."

As I began to preach, the crowd slowly calmed to a hush. "This is a new day for this city. You are not a forgotten people. The father loves you and sent his son, Jesus, for you. So many ask, why come to the Kingdom of God? When man sins, he rejects the ruler, the King of this Kingdom, Jesus. But to come under the rulership of King Jesus is an opportunity to restore your broken lives. The Kingdom of God may be invisible, but it produces things that are visible. Why come to the Kingdom of God? Come because there is love in the Kingdom of God. You will find peace, forgiveness and eternal life."

Masses of people flowed to the front of the audience during the altar call. The next day about 35,000 people showed up. The following day we met with every pastor in the city to discuss discipleship efforts for all the people who had responded to the altar call.

Our group could hardly believe what we were witnessing. It seemed only further proof that God had truly changed the city when the mayor turned the trash field into a plaza and community center the following year.

As I watched my dreams to touch the world coming true, I realized that I didn't have to wait 10 years to start a ministry. As soon as I returned from the trip, I registered our group as a non-profit. We quickly got to work on the next mission trips. We began hosting similar outreaches in cities all over Latin America sharing the same message of God's love and forgiveness.

Moving Mountains & Angel House Orphanages

During my time at Oral Roberts University, I never took the time to date. I was extremely focused on this burden for the world that God had placed on my heart. After graduation was another story. A passion began to grow inside of me. I could already see my life taking shape, and I wanted to share this deep love for God and people with a wife. I began to pray earnestly for my future with whoever she would be.

As I flew to Hawaii to speak at a conference, I gazed out at the waters of the Pacific, and my loneliness magnified. This conference with my parents was going to be amazing, but I yearned for that special someone by my side. My parents visited the Pastors and Christian Business Leaders conference each year and met up with old friends. While eating dinner on the patio of our resort on the first evening, another life-changing moment took place.

The resort consisted of five towers, all connected by waterways. Every 30 minutes a boat arrived, shuttling people between the towers. A boat pulled up as I admired the view. My gaze moved to a beautiful woman exiting the boat, and my first thought was, *That's the kind of girl I want to marry.* She had long dark hair and a beautiful smile. I just couldn't get myself to stop staring. I came to discover that her father was a pastor in Kansas City. I found this out because our parents happened to be close friends. We dated for a year before I asked her to marry me. A year later, we were married, and she has been my greatest support while traveling the world to share the Gospel.

Declare it Fearlessly

❧❧❧

The summer after graduation we held two massive outreaches in Nicaragua and Peru. We took 50 missionaries and more than 50,000 people showed up to each event.

As I sat in the Nicaraguan president's house at the end of our week, he stared at me in amazement. "Dominic, I have never heard of something like this before. You are so young, and yet more people came to the baseball stadium than have ever attended a political rally in this city. Even as you are praying for these people, they are getting healed. How is this happening?"

"President Bolanos, the scriptures read in 1 Corinthians 2:9, 'What no eye has seen, what no ear has heard, and what no human mind has conceived — the things God has prepared for those who love him.' God wants to absolutely amaze you. He has a passion and love for you. Your nation is experiencing this right in front of their eyes. I want to pray with you so that you, as an individual, may find God's love."

We bowed our heads as God's presence filled that office.

This would not be the last time I spoke with a president. We continued to reach Latin America with the Gospel, one city at a time. We held pastors conferences and received support from ministers right in their own city. Missionaries presented the Gospel and truth of salvation to every single school in the city. Dozens of mayors handed us the keys to their cities and introduced us to other political leaders. We chose neutral locations, like stadiums and plazas, and invited all the citizens to hear about the salvation Jesus Christ offers them.

Upon returning home from one of these trips, our team refined our model. Reaching an entire city for the love of Christ was completely successful. But as we hungered to reach more people, a question began burning within us.

I looked over at my closest team of missionaries and asked them, "What if we took this city model to the national level? What if we worked with every pastor in the nation? What if we built a mission team so large that they could visit every public school in the nation?"

In the fall of 2011, I met with Honduran President Portfirio Lobo to petition his partnership in reaching the entire nation.

"President, the scriptures ask in Isaiah 66:8, 'Can a nation be saved in a day?' What if this scripture is speaking to this part in your nation's history? I know that Honduras is in pain with unemployment rates at 40 percent. You are experiencing more violence than in any other nation per capita. What if all of your nation could be changed, healed, saved, in one single day? We have a vision to see exactly that happen." I paused as I watched the pensive look on his face.

He leaned forward, wanting to hear more.

Declare it Fearlessly

"We are going to call this 'One Nation, One Day.' We believe this dream is supposed to be realized in Latin America. We believe Honduras should be first. But we will only begin in Honduras if you agree to partner with us and agree to five terms."

I took a deep breath, knowing I was asking a lot. "Number one, we would like you to be physically present on July 20, 2013, as a formal welcome to the event. Number two, we want you to pass a bill through Congress calling 'One Nation, One Day' an official national holiday. Number three, we need you to pass a bill to allow us to bring an historic-sized mission team, 2,000 people, through customs and into your country. We want this team to be allowed into every high school in the nation to hold a one-hour school assembly the week before the event. Number four, we need Honduras to open up the ports and allow us to ship 18 containers full of books, aid, medicine, meals and shoes without any hang-ups or taxes. And number five, give us the 18 largest stadiums in the capital cities of all 18 states at no cost to us, and help us call all the people to the capitals."

Excitement charged the room as we discussed the plans. President Lobo signed the resolution committing to all the terms, and six months later, a bill was passed making all five terms possible.

In the next few years of planning, the mountains began to move. One miracle after another fell into our laps. In the past, to build a mission team of 200, I offered the opportunity to everyone I had ever met in my entire life.

Moving Mountains & Angel House Orphanages

Now we needed 2,000. Little by little, people from more than 20 nations began signing up.

We had only ever worked with two containers of humanitarian aid, and now we were promising 18. This monumental feat would require a large sum of money. But we knew God was much larger than our needs.

In order to get all of this done, we began trusting God not to let bureaucracy or our fears limit what we could accomplish. You see, what disturbed me and kept me up at night was the fact that the God who created the entire universe was available to us each and every day. He told us that nothing is impossible with him. We were still capable of more, if we just believed.

Two weeks before our trip, President Lobo and I met in Miami for a televised interview. The show aired on Telemundo across Latin America. The president and I met in the green room 10 minutes before the show began.

"President Lobo, I really want to thank you for taking a risk on me. You didn't know me, and I made so many promises and plans. I just really appreciate your trust."

"Dominic, I never took a risk. I knew from the beginning that this was right for our people. Tell me, what is 'One Nation, One Day' to you?"

Instead of waiting for my answer, President Lobo answered the question himself, "You know, this day will be a day of national reconciliation."

One of our biggest struggles entailed getting our team to Honduras. After talking to airport officials, it was concluded that Honduras could not receive a 747. The commercial airports in surrounding areas could not receive us, either. Everyone rejected us. The airplanes required level eight status, and the airline facilities were only level seven. We got down on our knees and depended on God. Before we knew it, the officials purchased extra equipment and extended the runway to become a level eight airport. We were able to fill a 747 three times and shuttled it from Miami. God brought hundreds of ministries alongside our team to unite for one cause.

On the day before the event, all of the evangelical ministers in the country came together in a spirit of unity to pray for the salvation of this nation.

That same day, I stood in front of a crowd of more than 1,000 politicians. "Yesterday, the old Honduras was a place of violence and division," I told the silent crowd. "I want to welcome you to the new Honduras. Tomorrow we will usher in unity, peace and prosperity. Your nation will experience a move toward non-violence." Before the end of our four-hour meeting, the group committed to the new Honduras.

On July 20, 2013, I faced a throng of 65,000 people in the San Pedro Sula stadium. Across the nation, 450,000 more were gathered in the other 17 states. "Welcome to the new Honduras."

A loud rush pulsed through the arena as they all stood in unison and erupted into applause and cheering for several minutes. The Honduran people were embracing the first day of their new nation.

As the night came to a close, President Lobo's words

from the green room hung heavy on my heart. I wanted these people to truly understand 2 Corinthians 5:18-19, which reads that "God has reconciled us to himself through his son, Jesus." I urged the crowd to reconcile with Christ.

"This is the day we reconcile with almighty God and each other. It's time to ask God for the forgiveness of your sins and a time to unite with one another in reconciliation. I want to ask you all to stand to your feet and join hands." The sound of thousands of people praying together was monumental. Even though every citizen may not have showed up to the stadiums, every public television and radio station aired the event.

Over the next year, we began receiving reports that violence in Honduras was dropping by nearly 30 percent. Churches experienced huge growth, and schools were being changed by the students' newfound faith.

ৡৡৡ

At this point, we are already entering into talks with other governments to orchestrate more "One Nation, One Day" events. We are also praying about taking the Gospel to the so-called 10/40 Window — the regions of Europe, Africa and the East between 10 and 40 degrees north of the equator, where poverty is greatest and access to the Christian Gospel most limited — and also Southeast Asia.

Some nights I lay awake in the dark, wondering if I am living up to the full potential of what God, the God who created the universe, wants to do with my life. He said that nothing is impossible with him.

There is still more that we are capable of, if we just believe. God told us in the scriptures that it only takes a mustard seed of faith to move a mountain. This scripture shakes me to the soul. God is not asking for Abraham-sized faith, or King David or John the Baptist-sized faith. God says that if anyone on the planet gives him his or her confidence and trust, he or she can experience a life where there are no limits. Giving God your whole life, putting all of your faith in him, means that you can say to mountains, "Move!"

If you live a life of faith, you will live a life where the rules don't apply to you, and you will be able to move cities and nations. As Peter walked out onto the water, I wonder if he looked at Jesus and thought, *If the rules don't apply to Jesus, do they apply to me?* Then suddenly he walked on the water, too. That is the unnerving invitation that every Christian possesses.

I live with this ominous truth every day. How much do I minimize what God really wants to do in and through my life? If there are a billion Hindus in India, if there are a billion atheists in China, if the Muslim Middle East is so cold and dark, what can I do? If God knows, God cares and God wants to change it, God, how can I give you as much trust as I have in my heart so we can change the world together?

Part II: Angel House Orphanages
The Story of Lindsay Russo
Written by Alexine Garcia

Dominic taught a five-session youth conference in Pennsylvania, and the teenagers vibrated with excitement. You could see that the testimonies and lessons they learned over the weekend were sinking in. The lead pastor brought us to the stage and talked to the kids.

"Dominic and Lindsay Russo have spent this time pouring into us. Now it is time for us to pour back into them. I want you all to gather around so we can pray for them."

My heart melted as the crowd surrounded us. They laid their hands on us, and the pastor prayed into the microphone.

When he finished, a 14-year-old boy grabbed me by the hand and looked into my eyes. "I feel God telling me that he is going to use you with orphans for the rest of your life."

His words nearly knocked the breath out of me, and I felt honored. I had never thought of or seen myself doing something like this, but I accepted his words as truth.

Five days later, we left for Kurnool, India, to start another outreach. We planned to reach the entire city and had our team set up to reach out to the community with presentations and humanitarian aid. Dominic started getting ready for the day, and I sat at the edge of the bed and watched him.

"I want to see an orphanage," I blurted out.

He turned around and gave me a critical look. *Are you crazy?* his eyes said. "Lindsay, this isn't exactly a tourist city. It's not really safe. On top of that, we have a busy schedule, and we didn't even make time for that."

"But don't you remember what that boy told me? I really think I need to see an orphanage."

He let out a deep sigh and sat at the edge of the bed next to me. He rubbed his forehead and began thinking.

"I'll see what I can arrange."

My doubts about the wisdom of the excursion deepened as we traveled farther down the deep, rutted dirt road, many miles outside the city of Kurnool, India. I suddenly realized that Dominic would probably not know our exact location if anything bad happened. Our driver finally stopped outside a tiny hut, and an Indian couple emerged to greet us.

"Thank you so much for coming. Welcome."

"Thank you for having us on such short notice."

"Well, the children are waiting, so why don't we go in?"

We walked through the couple's home and straight through the backyard to a small concrete building.

"This is it."

I had never been to an orphanage before, but this was not at all what I expected. We entered the tiny room. Thin children of all ages covered the dirt floor. Their dark skin and huge eyes staring up at us immediately moved me from doubt to compassion. So many kids crowded the little hut, we could barely move. Their clothes looked more like rags hanging from their skinny bodies.

I walked out of the hut and talked to the woman. "Who are these children? There are so many."

"We usually get around 70 a day. They are just street kids with no family. We don't have anywhere to keep them, so they just come here for the day and leave before night. As you saw, the road here is long, but they walk it every day. Some we see daily, and some we never see again."

I returned to the hut to play with the kids. We sang songs and laughed for a few hours before I had to leave.

ॐ ॐ ॐ

Back in Kurnool that night, I lay in bed staring at the ceiling tiles. The warm breeze flowed through the curtains. I could not stop thinking about all the children curled up in dirty newspapers right outside the door of our hotel.

I opened my journal and poured out my desperate heart. Prayers, plans, ideas to raise money, anything that I could do for these tiny children began to fill the pages.

Back home in Michigan, if you sat next to me on the bus, if you stood in line with me at the grocery store and especially if you were friends or family, you began to hear about Angel House. That was what I planned to call our orphanage. I believed that every child deserved a safe place to sleep. I imagined that each night angels would camp around this orphanage to protect the children.

I was so thankful that Dominic had the same heart that I did. We both agreed that if God provided the funds for this orphanage, we would build it. We cried out to him again and again for his help. *Lord, whatever you provide for this orphanage, we will give right back to you.* We applied our mustard seed of faith, and I continued to tell everyone I knew about the beautiful children in India who needed their help. We watched a miracle materialize as $25,000 accumulated. There are no words to describe what it felt like watching the money trickle in to fund this dream.

In December of 2010, I stood amazed in the doorway of our new orphanage as 50 children ran through the doors. They jumped on their new beds in excitement. Tears rolled down my cheeks as I watched a young girl hug her pillow. This was going to be the first night many of these kids slept with a pillow.

However, my excitement was short-lived. We had found a home for 50 kids, but 25 million were still going to sleep on their newspaper beds that night. Thoughts of rape, human trafficking and drugs bombarded my mind.

Back home, Dominic and I returned to our knees and petitioned God for help. This was the only thing we knew to do. Without the help of God, we could do nothing.

"We need nine more Angel Homes," a staff worker told us over the phone.

Moving Mountains & Angel House Orphanages

"Nine? We can plan four, but even that is going to be a huge miracle." Dominic hung up the phone, and I watched the pensive look on his face.

"We can build one with our own money."

"Lindsay, this is getting a little too big for us. Listen to what you are saying."

"No, Dominic, I know exactly what I am saying. We constantly trust God for citywide crusades. How is this any different?"

❧❧❧

God always answered our prayers, and he always provided for all of our ministry needs. But when it came to these nine orphanages, I never imagined what God had in mind.

"Please don't be mad at me, Lindsay." Michelle called me from our hometown of Kansas City. We went to high school together and had become close friends through cheerleading.

"What did you do this time?" I joked.

"I don't know if you are going to believe me, but I kind of signed us up for a game show."

"You did what?"

"Yeah, it's called *Minute to Win It.* The producer called me back today! It's not set in stone, and it might not even happen, but I wanted to warn you before they call to interview you."

My first thought was definitely not anger. Yet I didn't

visualize this as the opportunity it was. I saw it as something that would take time away from the important work I was doing.

Two weeks later, Michelle and I appeared on national television blowing bubbles, balancing objects with our mouths and solving puzzles to try to win a million dollars. We won $250,000, and as of this writing, we have opened 49 orphanages.

৵৵৵

Watching God use you to save the lives of thousands of orphans is a feeling I really have no words to explain. Our God created the entire universe, and he uses us as his tools to reach out to this lost world. This is our story, but God is writing one for you, too. This is your time to grab hold of that mustard seed of faith and start believing in everything that he can do in this world through you.

Commander's Intent
The Story of Dave Eubank
Written by Richard Drebert

"We will always stand with the oppressed.
Not because we are so brave, but because it is right."
Dave Eubank — Founder, Free Burma Rangers
(Speaking to a Tatmadaw Officer)

Warrior Born

Helplessly, I watched my squad of paratroopers bouncing across Georgia hardpan like ragdolls.

I drifted above my fellow U.S. Army Rangers swinging like a plumb bob, yanking and finessing my own parachute risers (controls), while treetops lashed the air in a 30-mile-per-hour crosswind. I weighed 145 pounds, and even with my M-16 and 70-pound combat load, the wind gusts slung me in wide, uncontrollable arcs.

RIP.

The acronym might easily correspond with my final jump in the Rangers Indoctrination Program. A tech had misread the anemometer (wind-speed gauge), and I was the last Ranger out of the C-130 troop door before a red light warned our jumpmaster to terminate the exercise.

All five paratroopers below me now lay like crushed insects, chutes flapping in unruly surrender.

Declare it Fearlessly

Landing flat-backed would stun me unconscious. It was likely that my chute would drag me, flaying my body on rocks and brush until some gnarled sapling impaled me.

A few feet above the earth I yanked one capewell (canopy release) on my chest to deflate half my parachute — but a crosswind gathered up every thread of silk, anyway. My flailing chute dragged me the distance of a football field until I jerked the other capewell and freed myself.

I lay on my back, stunned for a while, then gained hands and knees. My rodeo ride had ground my leather jump boots to shreds. Ammo, grenades, canteen and rifle were torn from my ruck, and Fort Benning grit had buffed my helmet to a bright sheen.

Two of my squad lay tangled in a wire fence, and three others rested in heaps of fluttering silk.

Suddenly the wind died to a zephyr. I was about to roll free of my fouled lines when a commanding inner voice overpowered my sensory forces, and I tuned in to *Someone* speaking quietly, yet cryptically — as when a father kneels before a child, eye to eye.

It's not your time, David.

I recognized the voice. I hadn't heard it so plainly in years. I rubbed blood from my eyes and hollered at the nearest injured Rangers, but no one answered. Soon medics arrived to bear away the wounded.

I was the only Ranger who walked away from our macabre drop zone.

Commander's Intent

While recuperating in my bunk, a scene in Thailand played in my mind — one that I had nearly forgotten. In it, I stood in my yard holding an open pocketknife, declaring to the world: "I'm gonna be a soldier! And then I'm gonna be a missionary!"

I smiled at my childish oracle. Lt. David Eubank would never be a missionary like his gentle, compassionate father.

I was born to be a warrior.

Sam Yaek

I clung like a hairless white monkey atop my wooden swing set, screaming at a scrawny, pointy-eared dog. The hound leaped for me, snapping at my dangling bare feet, and I felt myself slipping.

"DAAAD!"

Suddenly a black-and-gray cloud of dust swallowed up the red dog.

Duke, my German Shepherd, clamped the hound's throat in iron jaws, shook him unconscious, then pinned him to the dirt until he stopped breathing. Duke was my protector, patrolling the yard for snakes, and warning our family when anyone approached our home that was situated close to the Thai-Burma border.

I dropped to the ground and hugged my hero, my 5-year-old heart still beating in my ears. Duke sniffed the hound warily. It jerked a bit, and I ran to the house to find Mom or Dad.

Declare it Fearlessly

But Duke paid a price to rescue his boy. Red flecks drizzled down his fur where the rabid dog's teeth had nicked his shoulder. My family hoped that Duke might survive, but rabies symptoms developed quickly.

I experienced a sad *Old Yeller* day in Thailand. Losing Duke was my first lesson in what Mom called "suffering." She was my schoolteacher, and the Bible was my primer.

My 3-year-old sister, Ruth, my 2-year-old sister, Laurie, my dad, my mom and I lived in a two-story *Little House on the Prairie* home, about a day's muddy or dusty drive from Bangkok.

Missionaries Allan and Joan Eubank (Dad and Mom) had moved to the edge of the Thai jungle in 1961, just nine months after I was born.

Dad had been a Texas oilman and my mom a performer in Hollywood and Broadway before they answered God's call to be missionaries in Thailand.

My mother, Joan Hovis, had been singing with a USO troupe in Korea when she captivated my father with her beauty and Christian character. After sharing a cozy candlelight dinner and a single kiss, they sailed for contrasting destinies — though neither forgot their deeply spiritual connection.

Dad often received letters from London, Hollywood or New York, but he was resigned that Mom's dream was to become a star with her name in Broadway lights.

After Dad served out his Army commission, a sharply chiseled command from God blindsided him. Allan felt called to "be a missionary."

Commander's Intent

"Lord, I'm willing. But let me make a million dollars in the oil business — then I can go all out for you!"

College trained as an engineer and geologist, Allan Eubank worked for oil companies in Texas for a few years. He drilled ambitiously, but never felt God's endorsement on his plan to be a rich philanthropist.

Dad tossed his dreams of wealth to the Texas winds and chose to follow Jesus *without* qualification. He entered Brite Divinity School at Texas Christian University in Fort Worth, Texas, to prepare for missions work in Thailand.

"I was 28 years old and finally knew why I was born," Dad writes in his book *God! If You Are Really God!*

Then, in my father's third year at Brite seminary, Broadway star Joan Hovis danced into his life again. She "happened" to be performing at the Casa Mañana Theater, a mile away from where he lived. She starred in the musical *Oklahoma!*

Mom had been chosen for a Theatre World Award as one of the 10 most "Promising Personalities" on Broadway. But more than anything else, my mother wanted to serve God fully.

When she felt God speaking very plainly to her, "No one can serve two masters, Joan," my mother knew she needed to make some life-altering choices.

In her season of renewed commitment to Jesus, Dad began attending her performances at the Casa Mañana — and within weeks he won her heart.

Mom finished up her road shows with renowned

playwright and composer Richard Rodgers (of Rodgers and Hammerstein) to become a bride and missionary.

In 1959, Dad discovered the gusher he had always hoped for: Mom joined him in the adventure of a lifetime! With actors, soldiers and oilmen in attendance, Allan Eubank and Joan Hovis became husband and wife.

After mission studies, in 1961, Dad and Mom were ordained as ministers with the Christian Church Disciples of Christ.

Circling over Bangkok rice paddies, my father took my mother's hand and said, "I feel like we're coming home."

Mom smiled down at me in her arms and replied, "That's exactly how I feel, too."

At a village called Sam Yaek, about 50 miles west of Bangkok, my parents settled down to help plant churches in Thailand. Our first home was nestled in a valley of rice paddies, where years earlier, farmers had carved fields from lush forests of teak and bamboo. Sam Yaek served as my childhood FOB (forward operating base), and the miles of agricultural land became my "big game" hunting grounds.

"Look what I got, Mom!"

Exciting creatures crawled and flew everywhere, like centipedes longer than hotdogs, spiders with legs the length of my forearm and beetles that bounced off rafters like baseballs. Chickens, dogs, pigs and cattle scurried and wandered along worn footpaths, sleeping under the bamboo houses at night.

Commander's Intent

Villagers' homes around us were constructed with woven bamboo walls set solidly upon teak posts. To guard against flooding in the rainy season, each two- or three-room house perched about six feet or more off the ground. A set of teak ladder-stairs welcomed sandals or bare feet, and above it all, a family slept under a roof of thatch, palm fronds or tin.

Only one of Thailand's local denizens sent shivers up my boyhood spine. Bats flew into my loft bedroom from an opening in the roof. I recall their scrabbling claws on the ceiling and their flapping "capes." I spent restless nights worrying that they might drain my blood while I slept.

Although my family appeared typically American with conveniences like plumbing, the Eubanks' hearts grew more Asian year by year. Dad and Mom immersed themselves in our neighbors' culture and, for my sisters and me, English became our second language *after* Thai.

Along with schooling us kids, Mom included the local women and children in the chores and the challenges of her daily life. Her trained voice had serenaded thousands in Europe and the United States, but now she sang at humble gatherings of villagers, teaching them hymns like "What a Friend We Have in Jesus."

Dad mentored me in the traditions of his father, a Christian man of integrity, a veteran of World War I and a Texan through and through. Grandpa taught Dad to shoot a .22 rifle before he was 6 years old, and I hunted lizards, snakes and squirrels at a young age as well.

Declare it Fearlessly

I learned to swim like a jungle perch, and Dad nurtured my adventure cravings — Mom juggled evangelism work, keeping up with wash, dinners and chores, *plus* homeschooling a boy who daydreamed of killing tigers. Finally, my parents decided that I needed a structured academic environment.

Make-believe commando patrols at Sam Yaek ended when I was 7 years old. Dad and Mom enrolled me at the Chiang Mai Coeducational Center (CCC — later called the Chiang Mai International School), and loneliness for my family nearly broke my heart.

Jungle Boy in the City

Seeing Dad's wide smile and feeling his bear hug at CCC hurt worse now than waving from my train seat two months earlier.

I lay on a sweaty double bed with my father, staring at his thick chest rising and falling in the half light. Dad wasn't sleeping, either. He had driven to Bangkok and flown hundreds of miles to attend a meeting and see how I fared at boarding school.

My new home housed 27 students whose fathers were diplomats, oil company employees, missionaries and military liaisons.

The school building had been headquarters for the Japanese 7th Cavalry (an occupying force during World War II), and my first weeks at CCC were as close to torture as I could have imagined. I had buried my face in a thin pillow to keep anyone from hearing me cry myself to sleep.

Then came the dengue fever. My temperature climbed to 104 degrees, while inside my skull something hammered and poked until I vomited up *nothing* again and again for days. A nurse checked on me periodically, but most of the time I lay alone in my bunk while classes were in session.

This was the first time in my short life that I turned to God in desperate need. Shivering in afternoon sweats, I whispered to Jesus, "Mom and Dad believe in you, but they aren't here to pray. So, Jesus, if you're real, help me."

The moment I said "Jesus," a heavy cloud seemed to lift, and the room grew brighter. From outside of me, *Someone* embraced my sweaty body. His arms felt comforting, like my mother's, and suddenly I realized that I wasn't alone. God, whom my dad preached about and my mom sang about, was REAL.

I recovered my strength and began adjusting to living separate from my parents and sisters — when Dad showed up.

Lying with my father, homesickness reclaimed me, like the final act in a tragic play. I scooted against Dad and lay my head on his chest, weeping, missing my childhood in Sam Yaek. Dad came close to bundling me up and taking me home to my mom. But amid my grief and my father's empathy, God was engraving a detailed map upon our souls for his specific purposes.

Declare it Fearlessly

For eight years, Mom and Dad had journeyed by foot, and sometimes with an elephant pack train, preaching to remote tribes. They helped build churches, schools and handcraft co-ops and established prayer groups in villages.

Among ethnic tribes, the Eubank integrity and social standing blazed a trail for thousands of bold missionary and relief workers in years to come. And living in boarding schools at a young age tempered me for the mental and physical demands of my own unique calling.

At CCC, it took weeks, but my acute loneliness began to subside. During Thanksgiving break, my parents scraped together the price of a ticket to fly me home to Sam Yaek.

With my family and friends, Dad baptized me, affirming my trust in Jesus Christ, who promised never to forsake me.

In 1971, when I was 11, Mom and Dad, Ruth, 9, Laurie, 8, and my new baby sister, Suewannee, 2, moved to Chiang Mai, where Dad took a position at Payap University teaching New Testament and evangelism. Mom taught music and drama, and the six of us Eubanks were reunited!

I galloped my horse across acres of rice fields or climbed mountain passes around Doi Suthep, a few miles from our home. We filled up a whole restless, happy pew at our Chiang Mai church, and I couldn't get enough of *family*: Boy Scout camping, Mom's scrumptious dinners — and keeping pace with Dad as he visited churches in the hill country.

Commander's Intent

In Chiang Mai, as in Sam Yaek, the centerpiece of our social lives continued to be a weekly prayer meeting taking place in our living room. Neighbors gathered to petition God for healing sick people. Men or women troubled by evil spirits often asked my parents and their friends to help free them from demons, and my sisters and I often witnessed unexplainable supernatural events in the company of my father and mother.

At every opportunity, when Dad wasn't teaching at the university, he led groups at a blazing pace into the mountains to evangelize in villages. Dad was at war with the unseen world bent upon ruining the souls of men and women — but as a missionary kid, I shrugged off my powerful Christian heritage.

෨෨෨

By my last year at CCC, academics and sports only whetted my appetite for greater challenges, and one day an adversary showed up at school who was carved from the same Thai hardwood as I.

"I hear you think you're tough, Eubank ..." Pete Dawson smirked.

I was, but I was also a lightweight, so I always resorted to the same tactic on beefy opponents: shock and speed. Strike first — *hard.*

A fight with this new eighth-grader from the States was inevitable (students had been egging us on all day). I figured he would go down with my first strikes, and I could be on his neck with a chokehold in seconds. He would either give up or pass out.

At 14, I was the undisputed stud in my school, and there were several guys who would relish me getting thrashed unconscious. But I'd die before I let that happen. Pete was a wrestler and quarterback — and annoyingly good at talking smack.

I would enjoy this one …

I didn't answer Pete. I jammed my fist into his throat, and he hunched a bit as I slid behind him like a python. I hugged him to my chest, my arm squeezing against his windpipe. My power came from 20 pull-ups a day, so in cranking his thick neck, I expected him to drop to his knees, and he did.

But somehow he stood up again — with me hanging off his back. No one I ever fought survived my wiry-armed chokehold. Suddenly he lunged backward, slamming me against walls and concrete pillars, trying to break my hold — or my spine.

Pete introduced my head to every sharp edge in the room as his face grew red as betel nut juice, but he wouldn't give up! I figured if I could just hold on long enough … but I was interrupted. A few skinny teachers and a burly PE coach pried my locked arms loose.

After the usual scoldings and threats from teachers, Pete and I shook hands with iron grips.

You know, I think I like this guy …

And Pete was thinking the same thing. During our last year before graduating from CCC, Pete and I spent most of our free time in mock battles before or after school and on weekends. Our fights cinched a lifelong friendship (and paved the way for Pete to marry my sister Laurie).

When I left for my new boarding school, I was a sturdy 15 year old, about 5 feet, 8 inches, known around Chiang Mai as the farang (white boy) with a rifle. I said a respectful farewell to prayer meetings and church, ready to challenge the world with mind and fists at the International School of Bangkok (ISB).

Even the potheads worked hard to get good grades at my new boarding school. Airline CEOs, generals, ambassadors and diplomats sent their kids to the ISB, expecting sons and daughters to excel later at prestigious universities back in the States.

But at ISB, Pete Dawson and I grew tired of our bloodless battles. In our spare time we mixed with Thai gangs and challenged other young men from school to brawl on Bangkok street corners.

The local thugs were surprised that I spoke their language like a native-born Thai. And at the end of every successful fight, I locked in my memory the most effective, painful moves that weakened and defeated an opponent.

I excelled in sports, too, like basketball, but a love of fighting churned in my soul like Salween River rapids. No sport came close to the challenge and thrill of hand-to-hand combat. As a teenager, I learned that if I never gave up, no matter how bloody or beaten, I most often won in the end.

Declare it Fearlessly

Wounded Soldier

Confession is good for the soul ...

I sat slumped on Mom's sofa, head hanging like a dejected puppy. I had told Dad everything: my drinking Mekong sours (whiskey) with other farangs at Pop's Bar in Bangkok; my most recent altercations; skipping church; even my intentional fouls playing Singapore in the Thailand National Basketball Championship (we won).

"Let's pray about it, David."

Challenging myself at school or on the streets stole every waking moment and my dreams, too. I spoke to God seldom as a teenager, except when I went to church, but talking over my failings with Dad always seemed the next best thing to prayer when I came home on holidays.

I graduated when I was 18 and decamped to the States with a full ROTC scholarship. I enrolled at Texas A&M University, the same college where my granddad and father received their degrees in engineering.

Since high school, the ambition of leading men in combat had seized my heart, and my university instructors set my flight path toward an Army commission. I lived like a warrior monk, ignoring distractions like girls or parties. During college, I discovered mountain climbing, snow skiing, hunting and distance running. I spun on a breathtaking axis of adventure, with a long-term objective: to wear the green beret of Army Special Forces.

But in my early 20s, on the way to visit my family in Chiang Mai, a question came out of nowhere, like an RPG

Commander's Intent

(rocket-propelled grenade): *Will God destroy my map for the future?*

Officers had marked me for leadership and chosen me for Army Airborne School. I already wore paratroopers' wings in my third year of cadet training. But I knew the stories: God had turned my parents' destinies upside down. I worried about new orders that Jesus might give *me.*

Mom and Dad's prayer meetings started out as humdrum as I remembered, but out of respect I didn't flop on my bed upstairs like I had as a teenager. Instead, I reached deeply for some spiritual maturity — hoping to interact meaningfully with the powerhouse Christians who gathered there.

While mumbling along with the songs, some unsettling thoughts invaded my mind: *I've never asked if it was God's will that I become a soldier. Have I screwed up?*

"Is there anyone here who would like prayer about the future?"

Ian Talbot was a British missionary and pastor who worked with my parents, and I had known him all my life. I held my breath and lifted my hand.

Reverend Talbot placed his big hands on my shoulders — and gradually a flood of *something* enveloped me, like electricity reaching down to my toes.

I had *heard* about this kind of super-spiritual stuff, and I prayed — truly humbled.

"Lord, I'm so sorry that I didn't talk to you about what

I should do. I took the ROTC scholarship because I wanted to be in the Army ..."

God had been patient with me. He had allowed me to experience Army life, at least until *now*.

"Thank you for letting me be a paratrooper! But I give all that up for you, if that's what you want. I'll go to Africa as a missionary or *wherever* you say ..."

Reverend Talbot's voice broke through my whispered prayers, and I knew that God was speaking through him directly to me. I expected God to say that I was forgiven but to trade in my military books for a Bible. But that's not what God said.

"Keep doing what I have called you to do. I'm preparing you for service. You will face an event that will almost break you, but don't be afraid — it will not crush you. And, Dave, you'll always *know* when I'm speaking to you."

Nothing so "spiritual" had ever happened to me before. I came away from the Chiang Mai prayer meeting sensing my Commander's Intent (his overall purpose) and believing that God would unfold my destiny, mission by mission.

I graduated from Texas A&M and U.S. Army Ranger School as a second lieutenant.

I entered the Officer Basic Course at Fort Benning, training in tactics, mechanized warfare, aircraft control, weapons systems, communications, heavy weaponry, maps and compass, artillery, maneuvering forces, offensive and defensive movement and war games.

Commander's Intent

I wondered how God could ever use war craft in serving him — but I marched on his last orders. Fresh out of training, the Army shipped me to Panama, where I led a platoon of 40 men — my first command. I was 23.

In the Army infantry, extreme feats of strength and endurance get a soldier noticed, and I credit Mom's DNA from Granddad Hovis for my promotion to scout platoon leader.

In 1929, my granddad, Freeman Hovis, was a short, wiry "strongman" and a popular showman who toured the South as a bare-knuckle boxer, rodeo clown and singer.

My grandmother, Ruth, was a 17-year-old beauty who lived on a Mississippi farm. Ruth had just graduated from high school when my granddad, a charmer, came calling.

They eloped, and Freeman swept Ruth into a cross-country adventure. He performed in rodeos and sideshows before settling in Washington State and finally Texas. Ruth had two sons and a daughter with the strongman: Larry became a writer and movie producer, acting in the hit comedy series *Hogan's Heroes*. Michael became a movie producer as well.

But Freeman's daughter, Joan (my mother), was the star of Freeman's heart long before she was a stage sensation. The showman recognized talent in his adolescent daughter and drove her to perfection in dance and to near-perfect pitch in her singing. (To this day, Mom credits Granddad Hovis for her love of professionalism in the arts.)

I never met Granddad, but his legacy of endurance and

his demand for excellence in all endeavors flows in my veins — as well as his love for all things *risky*.

In Panama, in a 12-mile road competition, I carried a 40-pound rucksack in abhorrent Canal Zone humidity, breaking all records for speed — and my battalion commander noticed. Then I won the multinational Panama Stud Man Triathlon — and the commander called me to his office.

"Eubank, I want you to take over as reconnaissance commander for the battalion. You're our eyes and ears now."

Leading a battalion scout platoon, I applied my own unique strategies in jungle recon and felt the same thrill as street fighting in Bangkok. My hand-picked team dropped inside hot zones to map terrain, measure armed resistance or train local troops in guerrilla warfare.

෨෨෨

As an Army infantry commander, I had deployed with my platoon deep into the Peruvian jungle to recon and photograph major narcotics operations. Our extraction had been delayed, and my soldiers slumped against the vibrating fuselage in a C-130 examining toe blisters and dreaming about a bath after a month in the swamps.

But I held a penlight in my teeth, studying a topo map, plotting the next mountain I would summit. I glanced at my men, and no one met my eyes. They knew what I was thinking. They had more pressing engagements than rock climbing the first week back after a hard mission.

My mind tracked off the map for a moment as I thought about a young woman I had begun dating. Trish lived up to my officer's demand for visual excellence, and she seemed to embrace my Christian ideals. Admittedly, I was green as grass when it came to women. I romanced Trish like conquering a gendarme (mountain spire), ignoring every warning in the Bible about unequal relationships. After a short-range courtship, we tied the knot, and as in all marriages, the real Dave and Trish suddenly showed up. Trish struggled to meet my unrealistic demands, and it irritated me that our union was only a caricature of what my parents enjoyed.

I expected my wife to match my blistering pace in life, and she fell farther and farther behind. Our tempestuous union lasted only three years.

Moments after our divorce was final, I felt relieved because now I could pursue Special Forces action, unhindered.

I followed Trish out of the courthouse after signing the papers — and suddenly she stopped.

She said, "Dave, I'm so angry at you."

Dumb grunt that I am, I was shocked. "Why are you mad at me?"

Tears welled up in Trish's eyes. "You were not supposed to *let* me divorce you."

An avalanche of remorse buried me as I watched her walk away. I had failed to rescue Trish when she was falling.

Declare it Fearlessly

Alone in my apartment, the weight of my folly pressed me to my knees.

"Jesus, what have I done? Oh, God …"

Guilt beat me to an emotional pulp. I sobbed like a 7-year-old boy again, then took stock of my position: I had hauled a godless 50-caliber attitude into my marriage, and the knowledge of my shortcomings had arrived too late to rescue our relationship.

Even worse: *I had wrecked the integrity of my Eubank name.*

I made a new promise to consult Jesus in every decision I made, assuming that prowling jungles in war paint was all I would ever be tasked to do thereafter.

Burma in Brief

The year after my parents and I had arrived in Thailand, our neighbors in Burma (now called Myanmar) faced political upheavals that impacted people on both sides of the Thai-Burma boundary line.

During the '60s, while Allan and Joan Eubank sometimes traveled by pachyderm preaching about a God of peace, a new socialist dictatorship plundered the sovereignty of rice farmers and villagers in Burma. Resistance groups sprouted like bamboo shoots and cobbled together machetes and castoff World War II rifles to defend themselves.

A dictator and military general named Ne Win launched a campaign called The Four Cuts, designed to sever supply lines (food, funds, information and recruits) to guerrilla groups who opposed his Army, known as the Tatmadaw. Ne Win's Tatmadaw officers built permanent jungle camps from which his battalions terrorized families suspected of helping resistance fighters. Villages were systematically ransacked, then burned, the citizens enslaved for work projects.

After Ne Win, the Tatmadaw (Burma Army) steadily gained power under succeeding military generals. Tatmadaw tentacles reached into nearly every state in Burma, giving rise to more and more ragtag resistance armies, some as different in cultures as the monsoon and dry seasons.

In 1988, after quelling a democracy movement including Buddhist monks, college students, farmers and businessmen, the wealthy generals retrofitted their dictatorship, calling themselves the State Law and Order Restoration Council (SLORC).

They celebrated their power by renaming the entire nation "Myanmar." Ethnics in the resistance movements reject the new name, even to this day, refusing to wear the dictators' brand.

During the '88 democracy crusade, a few amateur journalists outflanked the junta, exposing the murders of thousands of protesters. And though major television networks were intrigued by dead bodies for a time, media spotlights never really penetrated the jungle warrens where orphans and uprooted families hid like animals from the Tatmadaw.

Declare it Fearlessly

In the '90s, the SLORC launched a fresh campaign of terror, burning villages and torturing headmen (mayors). Tatmadaw officers ordered homeowners to relocate to military-controlled settlements — bearing only what personal items a family could carry in a single trip.

A new day was dawning in Burma. Outside interests salivated over Myanmar's oil and natural gas wealth. Mining companies negotiated with the SLORC for rights to extract precious metals, gems and minerals. Burma Army battalions guarded foreign engineers who built dams to power industry — displacing farmers who had harvested rice there for generations.

China supplied armaments and training for Tatmadaw ground forces that grew to 400,000 strong. An appetite for heroin (chemically processed opium) in Asia and the West set Burma on course to be number two in global poppy production. Opium farmers harvested multiple tons of poppies in the remote Wa region (an area carved from Northeastern Shan State), along the China-Burma border.

The Wa government created its own armed force: the United Wa State Army (UWSA) to guard the sovereignty of their new Wa State. The UWSA negotiated a cease-fire with the Tatmadaw by paying tribute with opium and heroin.

As recently as 1979, Wa tribesmen had been offering demon spirits human sacrifices and performing latou (headhunting). At the same time, Wa Christians (descendents of converts of British missionaries) were building churches and seeing Wa hearts changed.

Commander's Intent

Only opium production propped up the frail Wa economy — and Wa Christians spoke out about the ruinous effects that narcotics had upon their society. Christians paid for their crusade with blood and imprisonment by secret police, but still they gained seats in the Wa government.

In 1993, the Wa State Foreign Ministry asked the United Nations for agricultural help to wean them off opium dependency. They planned to replace opium with crops like rubber, rice and tea. They also asked the United States to protect them from the Tatmadaw while they made the unpopular transition.

But to those in the region, it seemed the UN ignored their desperate pleas. And despite imposing an economic embargo, the U.S. government did not otherwise publicly get involved. The Wa delegation in Thailand informed Christian leaders in Chiang Mai about the rebuff and advised Wa ethnic leader U Saw Lu to speak to Pastor Allan Eubank.

By praying together in Dad's living room at Chiang Mai, my father and U Saw Lu shared in God's blueprint to bond a Special Forces officer and a special education teacher, who forged an alliance of love that would touch a nation.

Romantic Odyssey

Uncle Sam had assigned me to command joint exercises with the Thai Special Forces — and I was *home*.

Declare it Fearlessly

My altimeter read 20,000 feet as I leaped from a cargo door above our drop zone. I breathed oxygen through my HALO (High Altitude Low Opening) helmet, as well as a quick prayer for the Thai commandos I had been training.

In 1990, I had graduated from the Special Forces Qualification Course in the States, then followed up with elite forces training in survival and evasion tactics, resistance and escape and terrorism awareness. I also completed the Command Language Program and, later, the Command and General Staff College Program.

From a few thousand feet above my Thai team, I unfastened my oxygen mask and watched my trainees. Each soldier had reached terminal velocity and soared for several minutes before opening and navigating canopies for gentle landings in a designated rice field. I circled above them, relieved to see the open chutes, enjoying the agrarian view: green fields, villages, grazing water buffalo and farmers easing their backs as they waved.

High altitude parachute drops fed my hunger for adventure, and teaching Thai commandos the art of soaring under radar (in my backyard!) was a blessing straight from God.

Yet, even so, during this primo duty assignment, I struggled with God's direction for my life. I loved my work as a captain, commanding two A teams: one special reconnaissance detachment *and* my HALO detachment. Our missions were classified and high priority — but I couldn't shake the feeling that jumping out of planes and tracking down bad guys wasn't my purpose for living.

Commander's Intent

Humbled by my divorce and locked on stand down while the military mopped up after the short Gulf War, I returned to Washington State with two objectives: to serve a stint in the Middle East before the war was history and determine *exactly* God's will for my life.

And should I dial back my gung-ho intensity before looking for a relationship with a woman again? One thing I knew: Any woman I dated would be as sold out to Jesus as I was.

Erica was just such a young woman. I had known her since childhood, but after one ill-fated Yosemite trip, she decided that we weren't a good match.

She let me down easy. "But I know a girl who might actually *enjoy* this, Dave. You need to meet Karen. I'll introduce you …"

When Erica pointed me out to Karen Huesby, I had already been studying Karen during the church service like a book on a high shelf. I was still a little untrained in the rules of engagement, so I waited for a proper introduction.

"So. You're in the Army?" Karen asked me as Erica sauntered away with a self-satisfied look.

I suddenly floated above verdant fields at rice harvest. Karen's hazel eyes were captivating.

"Actually, I'm in the Special Forces," I managed to say.

I waited, but the words made no impression — she'd never heard of it.

"I'm a Green Beret. You know …"

Her polite headshake and smile said: *Nope. I don't.*

"Were you in the Gulf War?" she asked.

I changed tactics. "No, I was too scared …" Now *that* was a joke, and surely she would get it.

"You know. It's really *okay* to be scared."

It seldom happened, but I was speechless. The girl was dead serious!

We spent the evening with friends whom we both knew, and when I had interrogated her enough to discover that she was a devout Christian, I asked to see her again for dinner.

Not a chance, soldier.

She didn't say it that way, but I got the message.

Our odyssey of hearts might have ended that late evening, but I followed up with an invitation that piqued her curiosity. She had graduated from Seattle Pacific University, targeting a job as a special ed teacher, and she was growing to love the outdoors. I happened to be planning a technical ascent of Mount Shuksan in the Northern Cascades.

"You can stay at the base camp with friends while I do the hard stuff, or you can climb with us right to the top. Your choice."

"Can I bring a friend?"

I agreed, and six of us ended up preparing dinner and heading up the mountain at midnight when the ice was firm. It turned out to be an historic climb — for me. Three climbers quit after several hundred feet of using ice axes.

"You game?" I asked Karen. We stared up at a steep

wall of ice luring *me* to the summit. But what was Karen thinking? Her red face was beaming.

I snapped a climbing rope to the 100-pound blonde and started up, placing ice screws along the route and fastening her line to each one as protection from a slip. Karen emulated my moves, jamming crampons deep into the cold mountain face, until I paused to rest before the last push to the top. Before this final vertical climb I figured I should take stock of her mental state — it wouldn't be getting any easier, and we had a long descent to consider.

I stared down between my knees.

"So, how're you doing, Karen?"

Joy in her face lit up the whole mountain as she replied, "I'm diggin' this!"

I just shook my head. She seemed relaxed on her first technical ascent, like it was her 20th!

On our descent to base camp, I grew reflective. I told Jesus, "I'll do anything, Lord, if I can marry this woman."

But romance wasn't on Karen's mind — especially with a muscle-bound type like me. Karen had never dated before. She was probably waiting for a spiritual, patient, well-bred urban dweller to fall madly in love with her someday. Our personalities were so *different.*

I never sauntered anywhere, but marched — even in Walmart — always ordered by some inner mission. I was eight years older than Karen and on a rebound after a divorce. I could be opinionated and intense, but I was learning to be quiet and listen to a woman's heart.

Declare it Fearlessly

A man like me might threaten her objectives and confuse her emotions if she let him into her world. At least that's what she thought *before* God answered my prayers.

We never called it dating, but our relationship included hours of mountain climbing, skiing and long walks in the Washington forests. We started out inviting people to accompany us, but I whittled down our number of "chaperones," little by little.

As trust grew stronger, I poured out my heart to Karen, explaining the details of my mistakes with Trish. I bared my soul concerning my inner battle about remaining in the military. I explained how inadequate and tainted I felt when I considered pursuing Christian service.

Karen nurtured my desire to follow Jesus by listening, and without her, I might never have realized God's plan for my future.

As sudden as a flash flood, one day I decided to end my military career. I yearned for the satisfaction I saw in my father's eyes — a fulfillment never gained from my most daring Special Forces mission.

At 32 years old, I leaped into the dark to find my purpose for being alive — and I wanted Karen to go with me.

I applied to Fuller Theological Seminary in Pasadena, California, at the same time telling Karen that she was the one I believed God wanted me to marry.

But *my* adventure wasn't hers. She had achieved her lifelong dream to serve children as a special ed teacher in Seattle. God was using her gifts of patience, love and unshakeable devotion to help students with learning disabilities succeed.

My Eubank intensity frightened Karen, and she needed space to think about the whole situation.

"We need to stop seeing each other, Dave."

The heartbreak drove me to my knees. "Lord, if you want me to go to the mission field somewhere as a single man, I will," I prayed, but I hoped Karen would change her mind.

Months passed, and we spent time together at Christmas. I asked if we might start over. She said no.

I loved my Biblical studies in my first year at Fuller, but looked forward to spring break when I hoped to jumpstart Karen's interest. But during my visit to Seattle, I couldn't ignite a single positive spark.

Finally, I offered to chauffeur her to Los Angeles to see family, since it was on my way back to Fuller. She accepted the offer and busily packed her suitcases. We had one hour left before our drive. Soon Karen might ignore me for hundreds of miles with her nose in a book.

I wasn't going to waste a second of critical alone time.

I told her roommate, "I don't care who calls, I don't want to be disturbed …" Then I reconsidered. "The only person I'll talk to is my father …"

Dad never called me unless it was an emergency.

I took a deep breath and prayed one more time silently that Karen would have a change of heart — and the telephone rang.

Declare it Fearlessly

Burma Callings

"Dad?"

My father didn't dillydally. "Dave, U Saw Lu, who serves in the Wa Foreign Ministry, is visiting with me. He is here in Chiang Mai trying to get international support for a plan to transform the Wa economy. He wants the UN and our government to help them replace opium with crops like rubber and tea. They have refused, I'm afraid.

"He's asking for missionaries to come to the Wa State. He believes that only Jesus can change the hearts of the Wa.

"U Saw Lu noticed your picture on our wall — the one with your green beret. He asked if you were a Christian, and I explained that you were my son, studying at seminary. He asked if you would go to Burma and help the Wa people. I told Lu that we should pray about it, and we did — then we called you."

No mission from any commander ever gripped my soul with such authority. My answer can only be described as pure inner *worship*.

"Dad, how soon do they want me?"

I would be one of the first Western men to enter the Wa State in 30 years.

I hung up the phone.

"Karen, I need to talk to you …" I poured out my heart one last time. "I want you to marry me and come to Burma. I understand if you don't want to, but I really need you. One way or another, I have to go."

Commander's Intent

"When will you come back?"

I tried to keep my excitement in check when I sensed a crack in Karen's resolve. She never made snap decisions, and we were both caught in an emotional freefall.

"Three months. I'll be back for the new semester at Fuller. But if God has other plans, I may *never* come back."

I might be a celibate, single, lonely missionary in the jungle, for God only knows how long.

Like a check on ammo before a firefight, I breathed my commitment one last time.

I barely remember a single mile of our drive through Washington, Oregon and California. A quiet thrill stirred our hearts, like when Karen and I stared up at a pristine peak before a climb. As we approached Carmel, I suggested that we rest at the home of a sniper friend. He wasn't at the house when we arrived, so we killed time walking on the beach — and suddenly *all* of Karen's heart spilled out for the first time.

Her words tasted so sweet to my soul: "Dave, I don't want you to leave me, and I don't want you to 'never' come back!"

"Well, you've told me what you don't want. Tell me what you do want, Karen."

"I want you to follow God, Dave."

"Do you want to marry me?"

"Yes, but … can you let me sleep on it?"

For the first time during our remarkable courtship, I knew that Karen was mine. God confirmed it to me on the white sands of Carmel by the sea. By morning, God had cleared any clouds of uncertainty in Karen's heart.

I finished out my semester at Fuller in Pasadena, and Karen resigned her position as teacher in Seattle. Three months later, on a beautiful beach, my mother's powerful voice echoed in the cliffs of Malibu singing "Let Me Be Your Servant." My father performed our June wedding ceremony, and we celebrated with friends and family — the same month that the Wa leaders expected us to arrive in Burma.

We honeymooned twice — once in Malibu and again in Chiang Mai — before traveling by plane to the lawless Wa State in Northeastern Burma. After we arrived, we hefted rucksacks loaded with medical supplies and Bible teaching material, then traveled by foot and 4x4 truck (if available) to remote Wa villages.

With the help of Wa leaders, we silently skirted battalions of the brutal Tatmadaw and camps of the unpredictable United Wa State Army soldiers.

For three months of each year, from 1993 to 1995, Karen and I lived with Christian, Buddhist, Communist and Animist villagers desperate for medical and economic relief.

After our three summer trips, we carried back the dream expressed by Christian Wa heads of state: They prayed for the moral and financial backing from the nations affected by the scourge of narcotics. That was more than 20 years ago, and the Wa people are still praying for help.

Commander's Intent

And within this violent jungle frontier, the seeds of the Free Burma Rangers began to grow roots.

Victory Crawl:
Declare Without Excuse
The Story of Canisius Gacura
Written by Douglas Abbott

Closing my eyes was a mistake. I felt the blow before I heard the sound. The stick was thick and heavy, and the woman managed to strike my solar plexus with cunning precision. It felt like a battering ram had punched my stomach right through my spine and out of my body. I screamed, using the small amount of air left in my lungs, and twisted onto my side. I could not draw breath for long moments.

"Miserable little fiend! I'm getting tired of coming out here to pick you up." *Whack!* The stick hit me squarely in the arm this time, right on that bony part between the shoulder muscle and the tricep. I would have howled if I'd had the breath.

"Every time I have to come out here, I'm going to give you one extra lick." *Whack!* Pain exploded deep in my ear canal as the club struck my head.

"Please stop, ma'am! I am trying to hold on. Please do not hit me anymore. I'll stay up this time, I promise!" *Whack!* This time, the stick found a soft spot in my side.

"That's what you said last time. You are not only a cripple, you are lazy! Do you think I have nothing better to do? You'd better stay standing, or I'll beat you until every bone in your body is broken."

She hauled me to my feet and put my hands around two branches, stuck in the ground and nailed together at shoulder height. "Now hold on!" she snarled. Then she spun around and stalked back into the house.

Once she was gone, I permitted myself to cry. Things had gone from bad to worse. Since the illness came on, there was no moment, day or night, without pain. They called it "polio."

Every one of my joints felt like a red-hot poker had been jammed into its center. I could not walk or even stand. I vomited constantly, and sleep eluded me. Now I was being treated by a traditional healer who thought forcing me to stand up for hours on end was supposed to help. All it did was make my back and hips hurt worse, making me scream for hours. My inflamed joints did not allow me to hold on to the branches like I had been ordered. Eventually, my hands would grow weak from holding up all my weight, and I would fall to the ground. The healer's adult daughter spent her time arguing with her father and others. Eyes blazing, she would stomp out and start flailing me with her stick. I could not decide which was worse, her or the polio.

"What did I do to deserve this?" I prayed to God. "If you do not love me, why not just kill me?"

I had prayed such prayers before, but God did not seem to hear me. My body just kept getting sicker and sicker. Every time my father returned to check on me, I saw despair in his eyes. *He thinks I'm going to die,* I thought. *Maybe he is right.*

I gripped the branches as tight as I could and waited.

❧❧❧

My childhood was spent in the war-torn ruts of Uganda. My family had fled Rwanda's civil war before I was born, relocating to Uganda, but Uganda proved not to be a refuge. The same kind of wars erupted in Uganda as well, and my family lived in the most affected area. As we went about our lives and work, we had to travel through the bush in order to avoid the roads — and the ever-present soldiers, who went about looting, raping women and killing men, women and children without distinction.

As a young child, I witnessed horrific things. Once, a contingent of soldiers stomped into our living room, taking whatever they wanted. I watched one of them beat my grandmother savagely with his fists. They took every scrap of clothing my father owned and dragged him out the door with them, apparently believing him to be a rebel. We thought we would never see him again. Several weeks later, he was finally returned to us. He had been nearly killed.

Living in a very rural area, I was more frightened of cars than of wild animals. If I heard a car motor, I ran to hide. Also, the roaming bands of soldiers made the roads dangerous, so we used traveled jungle trails instead, which teemed with snakes, wild boar, elephants and leopards.

Declare it Fearlessly

It rained year-round where we lived, and sometimes the rains were so heavy, the water came down as from the spout of an enormous pitcher. It was like living in an endless puddle.

I was very athletic as a child. I loved to swim and climb trees and could run faster than anyone else my age. I was also a very hard worker. From a very early age, I wanted to *be someone*.

My father had three wives, who gave me more than 20 brothers and sisters. Each wife had her own hut in the area, where her children stayed. Our "village" also included grandparents, aunts, uncles and cousins. Our family business was livestock. One day when I was 7 or 8, I was out looking after some of our cows with my uncle, Kayitare. By midday, we became aware that two of them were on the verge of giving birth to their young. The onset of labor had occurred suddenly, and the births happened quickly. The newborn calves were not strong enough to walk the five miles back to our home.

"Canisius, we must carry these newborn calves back to the house," Uncle Kayitare told me. "Go, run home, and bring back several of your brothers. Hurry! And take the main road."

"No, I cannot," I insisted. "The jungle is safer. I will run swiftly."

Uncle Kayitare gave assent with his silence. I bounded off into the trees, intending to take a well-known shortcut. I did not give the weather a second thought; it was cloudy, but there had not been a drop of rain.

Victory Crawl: Declare Without Excuse

I saw the snake in the undergrowth just before I noticed several drops of blood on my foot. The pain came next — a fire that engulfed my foot and started moving up into my calf. Every time I glanced down, my leg looked larger with the swelling. Fear clutched my heart. The snake that had bitten me was a puff adder — its venom so poisonous that most people did not survive its bite. Each step now brought terrible pain, but I knew I had to keep running or I would surely die. I was still a long way from home. As evening began to fall, the clouds opened up, and in seconds I was drenched. The water came so fast and hard that soon little fountains of water shot up each time my feet hit the ground.

The downpour intensified, and so did the pain, which felt like a hundred hornets stinging me at once. Finally, I took to my hands and knees because walking had become unbearable. It was now fully dark. The rainstorm roared and swirled about me. The water rose, creating a river that edged higher and higher and tossed me around as though I were weightless. I was in danger of being swept away. At last, I clung to the trunk of a mango tree to wait for the rain to subside.

After what seemed like hours, the rain stopped and the water receded, leaving only the sound of dripping trees. I had been calling constantly for my father, but now I yelled with even more urgency. Incredibly, my father appeared from out of nowhere and gathered me up to carry me home.

"A snake has bitten me," I wailed.

"We will be home soon," he answered.

My leg was an awful mess. My father tied a rope around my thigh to prevent the poison from rising higher, but my frantic exertion in the jungle had done its work. The poison was well circulated throughout my leg.

Over the next couple of weeks, it became clear that the infection was very serious.

My grandmother, Maria, gathered herbs from the bush and smeared them over the bite, but they had no effect. My leg was rotting right on my body. The stench was horrible.

Meanwhile, the pain was unrelenting. I vomited constantly and ran a high fever. I was unable to sleep. All I could do was thrash on my bed while the skin of my leg darkened with the worsening infection. The wounds grew wider and wider, and maggots crawled in and out. One spot on the top of my foot grew wider. Several small bones in my foot came out, leaving a hole that went clear through my foot from top to bottom.

Finally, in desperation, my father grabbed a jug of pesticide used to kill the ticks that bothered the cows. He poured some of the poison into each of my open wounds, hoping to kill the infection. The burning was like nothing I had ever imagined. I screamed and screamed as the maggots tried to squirm away from the poison. The pesticide killed them but made the wound worse.

At last, my father guessed that only amputation could possibly save my life.

"I'm taking Canisius to the hospital," he announced.

Victory Crawl: Declare Without Excuse

"You cannot travel on the roads. You'll be killed," Grandmother told him.

"If I die, I die," he answered as he wrapped an old shirt around my leg. "I cannot let my son die. I have to help him."

My father owned a single two-seater bicycle that 40 of us shared. He picked me up, carried me outside and put me on the bicycle in the lap of my aunt, Priska. She held me steady while my father pedaled.

Much of the trip took us through the jungle, where my father had to steer around trees, shrubs, thorns and clumps of roots. He took shortcuts wherever he found them. The rest of the trip was on the roads, weaving around ruts and watching constantly for roving soldiers. In one day, from early morning until late evening, we made the trip. We had covered more than 80 miles to get to the hospital.

Surprisingly, I did not require amputation. I remained in the hospital for two months while my leg healed slowly. I was overjoyed to be walking again, though now I had a pronounced limp. I traveled to a nearby town with a medical clinic regularly to continue treatments, since my leg still had much healing to do.

One year after the snakebite, I was in town for a follow-up treatment, staying with relatives. During that time, another of my relatives' friends brought his son to stay there. The boy was deathly ill with measles and eventually died there in the house. Before long, I, too, was infected with measles. I had never had any vaccines.

Declare it Fearlessly

My father took me back to the same hospital — this time on a tractor. My father paid for the two of us to ride on the tractor's trailer, puttering and bumping more than 100 miles through heavy rains and washed-out roads. The tractor crept around meter-wide potholes, and due to recent rains, my father and I were constantly splashed with muddy water.

I was so ill that I remember little from that hospitalization, which lasted several weeks. However, I slowly regained my strength and eventually returned home, only to discover that, because of the bones I lost from the snakebite, my toes no longer touched the ground. I could no longer run swiftly. Many of the things I used to do without a thought — such as climbing trees — were now impossible. I was constantly afraid of re-injuring my foot, which was still not fully healed.

Three months after recovering from the measles, I strolled to school when I was overtaken by weakness and nausea. I could barely keep my balance as I walked along. After school, I returned home and played with some of my friends. At the time, I was in town undergoing treatments for my foot. I had in mind to push through whatever illness had struck. The following day, I was sent home sick from school. I rested that day and rose in the evening, still determined to push through. However, after playing for a bit with friends that evening, I became delirious with fever. As I lay in bed sweating profusely, I felt a terrible pain in my joints. It felt as though skewers had been jammed into every joint in my body. It was horribly painful. I could not move without fire shooting through my joints. I vomited in my bed all night.

My father was away and did not return for a week. My caretaker brought me to the clinic, but they could not determine what was wrong. Finally, the doctor ran some tests and came back into my room clutching a chart. He made the somber pronouncement: *polio*.

The healthcare workers made me as comfortable as possible, but they could do nothing about my illness. They recommended I be brought to a "traditional healer" — similar to a witch doctor. The healer examined me and declared, "I'm going to help him immediately! If you give me a cow, I will treat your son."

My father acquiesced. "If you need two cows, or even more, I do not care. Just help my son!" he said.

The healer made cuts in my flesh to draw blood, which he rubbed onto a leaf. Then he ground up various herbs and smeared them all over my body. I got the impression he was making things up as he went along. Eventually, he told me to stand upright for hours at a time. This was enormously painful, and because of my severely weakened legs, I required help. At other times, the healer tied my arms to tree limbs. At still other times, I had to try to hold myself up by gripping the branches. I was far from home, and my father and relatives were able to visit only occasionally. I felt so alone.

Through this entire ordeal, I began to despair of recovering. I sensed my illness was wearing my family down. My father and many of my brothers and cousins had gone to great lengths to help me through three major illnesses, and instead of getting better, things kept getting worse.

Finally, the healer admitted he could not help me. "Take him somewhere else," he told my father. I began to wish I could die. My body shrieked with constant pain. I could not sit or stand without help.

My father brought me to a different traditional healer, who gave my father the same flamboyant assurances: "In one week, your son will be walking!" I was encouraged, but my enthusiasm quickly deflated when I found myself going through the same things as before: holding myself up for hours on end, falling to the ground when I could no longer hold on. This new healer had a miserable daughter whose job it was to check on me. Each time she found me crumpled on the ground, she would run up and beat me with sticks as though I had done something wrong. This occurred whenever my father was absent, which was most of the time.

I began to ask God hard questions: "Do you love me or care about me at all? Do you even exist?" I began to believe that God hated me. It seemed the only explanation for the horrible things that were happening.

"If you do not stay upright, we will not take you to the toilet!" the healer screamed one day when he found me on the ground. My high fever made me constantly thirsty. In spite of the pain in my joints, I painstakingly crawled outside the house to relieve myself. The doctor and his daughter found the mess and screamed at me. After a few repetitions of this, I resolved not to eat. I reasoned that if I did not eat, I would not need to use the toilet. All the time, I grew more and more bitter toward God.

At last, the healer told my father he, too, had failed. "Take him home, and wait for him to die," he said.

My father was deeply discouraged. It had been a full year since I had contracted polio, and I was as bad off as ever. All I could do was lie on the floor. I needed help for everything. No one could look at me for long without bursting into tears. They lost total hope. I was the first disabled person in our whole community. No one understood how to treat a disabled person.

Unexpectedly, I began to recover. I regained the ability to sit, then I learned to get around by scooting backward on my bottom. Eventually, over the next few years, I learned to crawl. It was a vast improvement, but it came with a price. Soon I developed deep wounds on my knees and feet that never healed. I tore them open constantly on stones, brambles and roots. The wounds constantly became infected as I dragged myself through mud and puddles.

Polio had effectively ended my education. I had attended only four months of school before the disease struck me down. I felt like I became something marginally humanlike — a gnarled, pitiful creature who moved on the ground with grotesque open wounds. Not only could I not attend school, but none of my brothers would even allow me to touch their schoolbooks. "You're so filthy, you can't touch our books," they said. I was constantly covered with mud from crawling everywhere. People suggested I learn to shine and repair shoes since I would not be able to do anything else.

At the young age of 13, I despaired of ever having a satisfying life. Who can be content if he is not loved or respected? I was neither. I was half a person — an invalid in body and spirit. What woman would have me? And how could I ever care for a family in my condition? At the same time, I was not blind; I noticed every beautiful girl who went by with a terrible longing. My many afflictions had not expunged the desire of my heart for a soul mate. But it could only be a pipe dream — one that would eventually make me even more miserable, if that was possible.

All things considered, there was no reason for me to exist. I had no friends. My family, so helpful during my illnesses, had given up on me once it was clear I was permanently disabled. I had become like a dead person to them.

Strangely, even as I grew increasingly despondent, I continued to speak to God, as though none of my dark ruminations could succeed in overturning my conviction that there was someone up there, as unjust as he might be.

"God, are you real? Do you hate me? Why? What crime have I committed? How can I ever have a life? Is it your habit to create people just to watch them writhe in torment? Does my pain bring you some perverse satisfaction?"

People told me God had let these things happen to me

because I was a bad person. But I had seen bad men. I had watched men with rifles take the virginity of young girls, murder children and even throw infants onto bonfires. Did God think I was going to become like them?

Through all my turmoil and anguished prayers, I found no comfort and heard not a whisper back from God. It was as if his face were turned forever away from me. It felt like a colossal injustice and kept me continuously angry. Perhaps God was my enemy. It was the only thing I figured explained the events of my life, but it also cast a deep shadow over my future.

I forced myself to smile during the day and cried myself to sleep every night.

I entertained frequent thoughts about suicide, first offhandedly, then with a morbid intensity that grew steadily. It did not help that others agreed.

Once, a family friend came to visit. He had not seen me since before my troubles began and remembered me as a hardworking boy. I overheard him speaking with my grandmother.

"He's a good boy, but it might be better if he died," the man said, chewing a bite of food. "He makes people sad to see him, the way he's almost too weak to sit up. He is in obvious pain. People probably cry just to see him."

Each time I heard comments like this, I felt more certain that there was no reason for me to be above ground. It hurt terribly to hear them. Often, despite the pain, I would sit motionless for hours so out-of-town visitors would not notice my condition, how I crawled, and make cruel statements that hurt my heart. Shame filled me when I was forced to move around and people could see.

Finally, the scales were tipped. I dragged myself an entire kilometer through the brush to a community well. I pulled myself up on the stones and was on the verge of throwing myself in when a neighbor approached me.

"What are you doing?" he asked, walking toward me.

"I'm waiting for a friend," I lied.

"No, you're coming with me," he said. He lifted me off the wall and walked alongside me as I crawled home. Some weeks later, I went back to the well to finish the job. However, just as I climbed up to dive into the well, another neighbor came up and did the same thing.

I did not permit myself to consider the significance of what had occurred at the well. I wanted to be out of this world, one way or another.

It was the year 1991 when I picked up a two-liter jug of pesticide and prepared to drink as much of it as I could. This was the same substance my father had poured over my snakebite wounds. There was little doubt that it would do the trick. The difficult part would be getting it down.

I wrapped trembling hands around the bottle, lifted it from the ground and was about to raise it to my mouth. Just then, I heard a voice inside me say, *If you do this, you will die.* I set the bottle down for a moment. I was terribly afraid and began shaking profusely. I felt a deep conviction. For the first time, I felt that it would be wrong to kill myself. The voice said, *You need Jesus.* The voice

Victory Crawl: Declare Without Excuse

was so clear that it might have been physically audible. For three weeks, I continued to hear the voice and those words reverberate inside me: *You need Jesus.* After hearing this over and over, I finally decided to attend services at a nearby Christian church I had been acquainted with previously, where my aunt, Jane, attended.

The church was two and a half miles away. I crawled the whole distance. When I arrived, several ladies sat preparing strips of thatch to repair the leaky roof of the building. I offered to help and dragged myself up onto the roof. As I applied the strips to the holes, the ladies stood below and smiled up at me.

"You are building the house of God," one of them said. "It is a prophetic word. You have served God even before he is in your life. You will serve God in your life."

I had said nothing to these ladies about the voice I had heard and the words echoing in my head for three weeks. It was yet more confirmation, as if I needed any. I decided, *From today, I'm giving my life to Jesus.*

I smoked my last cigarette and gave the pack to the woman who had spoken to me. "Madam, I'm going to walk with God from this day on." The pastor took me into the church, where I met Jesus, the one who made all the difference in my life.

It was a Friday when all this happened. I called it my "Good Friday," and it was better than I had known a day could be. I felt love and joy that day that had not seemed possible. It was as though God was assuring me that I had done well. My insides soared.

Declare it Fearlessly

I stayed at the church that entire weekend, helping with work projects and attending services. As I had promised, from that day on, I walked with God. I crawled to church five miles roundtrip every Wednesday, Friday and Sunday for services. No matter what the weather.

I developed a passion for being in God's presence, which I found whenever I did his work. A devout Aunt Jane occasionally carried me on her back so I could go to overnight prayer. I longed to go with my church fellows on their evangelistic outreaches, but I knew I would slow them down. "I will stay and pray as you go out. That will be my contribution." And so I did.

I wanted to help my church in other ways, but the others would not let me. So I started dragging myself there early in the morning to sweep out the church building. Afterward, I crawled up and down the benches and papyrus mats, praying for the people who would sit there. "If anyone comes with a problem, please help him or her."

In late 1992, I began to ponder a new idea. If I could find some large rubber boots, perhaps I could slide my knees inside them to protect my knees and feet as I crawled. One day I came across a great treasure. A pair of black rubber boots, badly torn, that someone had thrown away! I took them home and spent days by the fire with a hot knife, sealing the tears and holes. Those rubber boots became so precious to me, a gift from God to help me do the Lord's work more easily, and they helped me stay more neat and clean despite having to crawl.

I began to fast and pray, asking God for an

opportunity to read his word for myself and serve him in ministry. My education so far consisted of four months of elementary school. In 1993, I joined a school at an orphanage that housed and fed 400 children orphaned by the war. I crawled half a kilometer each day to attend school there. On my first day of school, the entire school came out to watch me crawl down the street on my way in. They were amazed.

"What does he have, six legs?" one little boy said with a laugh. My boots made it look like I had an extra pair of feet, and the children wondered what I was hiding inside them.

I had much learning to catch up on. I was assigned to the kindergarten class, but I begged to be placed with the second graders. "I'll work hard," I said. "If I fail, then put me back in kindergarten." One of my new little friends held my hand to help me form my letters. I was 15, and my baritone voice made a startling contrast against all those second grade sopranos! I advanced rapidly, learning to read and write in three months, then continuing on through the higher grades.

I found wonderful fellowship there at the orphanage. It was like coming home to a family I'd never had. The staff even invited me to live there, which made my life a great deal easier. Now, to go to school, I only had to crawl from the dorm to the classroom. As I learned to read, scripture became real, and I trusted God more and more. I told everyone about God as I crawled along.

The orphanage was run by a wonderful missionary

couple, Lovie and Syvelle Phillips. Lovie helped me gobble up the foundational curriculum in the ascending grades of school. More than anything else, my desire to learn was attached to my goal of being able to read God's word for myself. With Lovie's help, I ascended through primary and then secondary school and finally looked forward to Bible college. I was amazed at how far God had brought me in such a short time, and I always tried to make God my number one priority. Meanwhile, I was still impoverished, so much so that I had no wheelchair and continued to crawl everywhere. Wherever I went, I spoke to everyone who would listen about how much Jesus had done for me. However, my precious black boots were beginning to fall apart again.

One of the directors of the orphanage, Pastor David, was a great intercessor. He challenged the local church I now attended to chip in to buy me a brand-new pair of boots. The congregation was very poor, but they gave all they had to purchase the boots for me. What a wonderful feeling it was to slide those new boots on for the first time!

For a time, I thought a great deal about the possibility of being healed. I was no longer angry about my physical limitations, but I was weary. I felt I was less than people who still had their mobility. I watched God heal others miraculously and prayed fervently for him to heal me as well. "God," I said. "I know you have good plans. Would you let me be able to walk?" I thought if I became a minister, no one would receive my words once he saw me crawling.

Victory Crawl: Declare Without Excuse

Finally, God told me, *I healed you from the greatest disability you ever had — the one in your soul. I am keeping you as you are so people will see I do not play favorites. Go and preach!* So I dragged myself through the dark and the mud and prepared for ministry. Soon, I began to be invited to churches to speak.

When I spoke, people repented. I began to see that, regardless of my faculties, I could fulfill an important role in life. I began to tell myself, *I can be someone. I have value.* The words were incredibly uplifting to me, all the more because I believed them.

From my speaking engagements grew many other opportunities. I became a youth leader for the whole primary school district. Then I became a student leader in the secondary schools and was invited to speak at conferences and seminars.

The year 1998 brought one of the greatest moments of my life. Lovie and her husband presented me with my first wheelchair, which they purchased from an American company. It had a purple finish, which Lovie explained they chose so that every time I looked at it, I would be reminded that I was a son of God, the King. It was the finest wheelchair I had ever seen in Uganda, and it helped me immeasurably in my life and ministry.

I thought, *Now I will never have to crawl again.*

However, God had other plans.

I was accepted into Yesu Kwagala Bible College in the year 2002. This was a dream come true that had seemed impossible. The administration initially told me that as a wheelchair-bound person, I would be unable to contend with the school's undulating topography. The school was at the top of a steep hill, with the student quarters at the bottom. I was faced with a choice: give up my wheelchair, or give up my dream of Bible college. Rather than forfeit the opportunity, I returned to crawling for four years. This was no light decision.

The first week, a kindhearted instructor stopped and drove me to the top of the hill each morning. However, after that first week, I was left to my own devices, which meant crawling up the steep slope and back down every single day.

I had become accustomed to the relative ease of traveling in a wheelchair, and I was not particularly keen on having it taken away from me. Besides, the hill was long and dreadfully steep. Even more difficult was the length of my matriculation, an entire college career that stretched ahead of me. Could I really keep this up for four years? Was I willing to? It was a moment of truth.

I wrestled with God in prayer. "Are you punishing me?" I asked him.

God answered me with a question. *Do you think you will be blessed when you are complaining? Did you come here to be driven or to let me work in your life? I have plans for you. This time has a purpose.*

This went on for three days. Finally, I prayed, "Give me grace to serve you with joy." From that time on, I chose to forget about my feelings and accept my circumstances. I chose to pray for those who passed me by on two good legs, instead of wallowing in jealousy. By God's grace, I crawled up the hill to the school every day, even in the pouring rain. I never missed class.

I finished my studies there with a bachelor's degree in theology in 2005. I knew I wanted to be a pastor, and I had in mind to reach out to disabled and impoverished people. I knew their lives, how hopeless many of them felt as they lived on the streets begging, drinking and doing drugs. I fasted and prayed every morning for direction from God.

But God told me, *Go to Rwanda.* As I had at many other times, I wrestled with God over this directive. I had never been to Rwanda. Many of my family had died there. Language was a barrier. I loved my life in Uganda, where I had scores of friends who loved and respected me. I had nothing in Rwanda. Yet, God said, *The best place for you to be is in my will.*

After several preparatory trips, I packed up everything I owned and traveled to Rwanda, which I dubbed my "promised land." In December of that year, I started a church in the living room of the cheapest house I could find. The house was sturdy, however, the road to reach it left much to be desired. The street was steep, full of bumps and featured a trench of constantly running water. Impossible for my wheelchair.

Once again, I had to resume crawling. I felt my affliction was a sworn enemy that managed to find me wherever I went. But God spoke to me again. *I don't need your strength. I want your obedience.*

I was learning that obedience to God was a course

laden with adversity — and risk. It was illegal to hold church in a home. The police came to shut us down many times. Each time they came, I implored them, "Give us a chance. God told me to come here to help these people. Once I walked like you. I'm doing something to help my people, speaking hope and life to them, sharing my pain, my heart. I'm not stopping. That's God's business." Finally, they left us alone.

The next thing was to pray for land. It wasn't long before God answered. *Yes, I will give you land.* It was difficult to take him at his word, when I could barely even pay for food.

However, in faith I announced to the church, "God has given us land."

I found a nice plot of vacant land and believed this was the land God had spoken of. The entire church came out to see the property. We stood on the tract and prayed over the spot, but we still had no money. "If God spoke, he will make a way," I assured them.

I prayed over that land for one year. My pastors, Pastor Ron DeVore and Pastor Steve Mayanja, visited our church in Rwanda and prayed with me. They stood with me and supported me in the vision for the Rwandan church. They shared the story with their supporters when they went home. Among those supporters was a couple who were amazed to hear the story of how I had crawled to class for four years in Bible college. They felt moved to donate $21,000 to us for the land.

Meanwhile, I was preparing for my wedding. I had

been praying for a wife and family since 1994. In 1998, God had promised me a wife one day, so I considered the matter closed with regard to the thing itself. However, timing was another matter. I spent the next seven years wondering when she would come along. Then, in 2005, I was working in a church and noticed an attractive young woman named Ellen who led the worship. At the time, all I thought was, *I wish she would lead the worship here permanently.*

Sometime later, I was praying one night, and as was often the case, my prayers got around to the subject of my future wife. *Don't you think Ellen would make a fine wife for you?* God said as I was praying.

"No," I answered and kept praying. However, the next time I was at church, I noticed that Ellen had a passion for Christ and strong convictions. Moreover, now that God had introduced the idea, I found her very intriguing. However, I felt sure that she would not want someone like me for a husband. My heart was pulled in both directions. Finally, I resolved to share the idea of marriage with her.

"I'm not forcing this on you. You are free to say yes or no," I told Ellen.

"Give me some time," she replied.

One month later, Ellen approached me at the church. "Pastor, I'm saying yes to you."

"Why?" I asked her, incredulous. "Haven't you noticed how I drag myself around everywhere? My church is in the living room. Whether I walk or don't walk, are you willing?"

Declare it Fearlessly

She smiled a gentle, beautiful smile. "Come to me the way you are. I accept you. Before I met you, God spoke to me about you. 'This is your husband,' he said. I didn't believe him, but God persisted. I asked God to have you speak to me, as a way of confirming what he had said. You did exactly that. I will be your wife."

We decided to get married in Uganda near my home. When we planned the wedding, we invited everyone, even those who had thought I'd never amount to anything. The day we were married, more than 500 people heard the Gospel. In a divine unfolding, newspapers and radio stations picked up the story.

No one thought I could have a child (not even me!), but when our firstborn son came along, no one could deny what had happened; the child looked exactly like me! But he wasn't disabled, as many had predicted. He runs like the wind, just as I did once. Since he was born, Ellen has given birth to two more sons and a daughter. I am astonished that God gave me a family — a first-rate one at that! To this day, I look at my beautiful wife and four healthy children and marvel at God's provision.

My church is in Kigali, Rwanda — a city of one million people. We have two campuses, one of them in an area where Islam is predominant, the other in a section devastated by genocide. The original campus is in a neighborhood whose name translates to "the place of dead bodies." I went against tradition and named our church Nyabugingo Worship Center, which means "life-giving worship center."

Victory Crawl: Declare Without Excuse

Our ministry includes crusades, conferences, village outreaches, a food program that benefits 200 children, seminars, a weekly radio show and many other outreaches — including outreaches to those with disabilities.

When I look back, I regret that I spent many years hating my disability. I swallowed whole the message of the world, which is that strength, physical beauty and personal abilities make someone valuable. But God showed me that my disability is precious in the heavenly economy. I take comfort in the words of the Apostle Paul: "Three times I pleaded with the Lord to take [my affliction] away from me. But he said to me, 'My grace is sufficient for you, for my power is made perfect in weakness.' Therefore I will boast all the more gladly about my weaknesses, so that Christ's power may rest on me. That is why, for Christ's sake, I delight in weaknesses, in insults, in hardships, in persecutions, in difficulties. For when I am weak, then I am strong" (2 Corinthians 12:8-10).

Countless people have expressed amazement at what I have accomplished. I once spoke to a group of young people who took turns asking me questions about my ministry and how I have been able to do what I have done.

"Are you surprised at what has happened to you?" a soft-spoken lad in the front row asked.

"Oh, yes! Back when I was crawling, I couldn't even buy sandals. But God said, 'I will send you to the nations.' I didn't believe it. But God is a real God. If we say yes, he's going to work in our lives."

"Why do you work so hard?" a pretty girl asked.

Declare it Fearlessly

"I wasted much time in sadness. Now I want to serve God. Besides, I do not work with my strength, but with Christ's power!"

"You seem so happy and confident for someone disabled as you are," another girl said. She smiled broadly.

I grinned back at her. "My confidence and joy come from knowing the Creator. We are fearfully and wonderfully made. My outside appearance doesn't show that each of us has hidden treasure. We can't discover God's richness until we dig the treasure out."

"How do you explain the success of your ministry?" asked a well-dressed young man.

"Obedience is so important. It's foolish to the world, but means everything to God. A single step of obedience can accomplish wonders. Consider David's obedience when his father said, 'Check on your brothers.' He took one step and did that one thing, and it led him to Goliath, which was the event that turned him into the king of Israel! The Lord himself tells us this in Zechariah 4:10: 'Do not despise the day of small beginnings.'"

A shy girl in the back raised her hand. "My father told me that you recovered from the bite of a puff adder. Weren't you supposed to die?"

This was the question I had been waiting for. I nearly shouted, "Nothing can kill you when God has his hand on your life!"

Ten Words
The Story of Reverend Rob Schenck
Written by Arlene Showalter

"Rob Schenk." I shook the stranger's hand.

He introduced himself as chief of staff for a U.S. senator.

"It's a pleasure. I look forward to our conversation."

We moved straight to the issues facing our nation in 1995. Within minutes, I realized my companion and I stood as far apart on the subject as pro-life and pro-choice factions on moral absolutes. My viewpoint stemmed from my relationship with God and my understanding of his laws. I wasn't sure yet what defined this man's morals.

At first, we spoke alien languages. I sought common ground. *The Ten Commandments. Most Americans know about them one way or another.*

"Are you familiar with the Ten Commandments?" I asked him.

"Well, sure, yeah." He paused. "I don't know where or how I learned about them, but I do remember some. Thou shalt not kill. Thou shalt not steal. Something like that and more."

This is my starting point. I sensed God leading me. *Use the Ten Commandments to bring the Gospel to the D.C. community.*

Declare it Fearlessly

྾྾྾

"Train a child in the way he should go,
and even when he is old he will not turn away from it."
(Proverbs 22:6, God's Word Bible)

"Kike! Christ killer! Dirty Jew!" Dad heard these slurs, punctuated with clenched fists, while growing up in 1930s New York.

In his late teens, he went to a dance in Harlem, met and fell in love with a black girl.

"I want to marry her," he confided to a friend.

"You do and you'll be killed."

"Because she's black and I'm not?"

"Exactly."

She can't help being born black any more than I can a Jew. It's not fair.

They didn't marry, but Dad did join the NAACP as soon as he turned 18. His aversion to prejudice drove him the rest of his life.

World War II invaded America. Dad's brother, Robert, flew a B-17, determined to stop the Nazi hate regime. Dad followed the war's progress through the news and learned about the Holocaust. He began keeping a scrapbook of newspaper clippings.

Mom experienced a different form of prejudice from her youth. Struck with polio when she was 6, she lived out the rest of her life with one underdeveloped leg.

"Gimpy!" kids taunted as Mom hobbled past them.

Ten Words

They slapped her books out of her hands and often knocked her down.

Although disabled during a time when no accommodation was made for her, Mom married. The union produced two daughters.

Then her husband, an alcoholic, committed suicide. Mom lived under the triple shame of disability, single motherhood and widow of suicide.

One day, as she folded clothes in the laundry room of the townhouse complex where she lived, a stranger walked in. A few minutes later, she collected her baskets and turned toward the door.

"Please, allow me." The man moved between her and the door and held out his arms.

Mom felt shock and disbelief and gratitude at his gesture.

Dad seemed oblivious to Mom's physical imperfection and could not know the internal shame she carried. She fell in love with that stranger, who showed kindness and lacked prejudice.

Dad reciprocated her love.

His family's reaction was explosive.

"You will marry a gentile?"

"No way."

"We cannot support this union."

"Nobody will attend your wedding."

"You will be an outsider to us."

Dad reeled under the familial onslaught.

"Don't worry, Henry." Mom, although born Catholic

and raised Episcopalian, had lost her faith when her own mother died while Mom was in her teens. "I'll convert."

"It means you must pledge to raise your children Jewish."

She shrugged.

"I will. I'm being practical here."

They married in 1956.

Two years later, for reasons known only to him, God chose to split a single fertilized egg that became my identical twin, Paul, and me. From sharing a womb until today, we continue to work side by side.

❧ ❧ ❧

"Silence in the face of evil is itself evil:
God will not hold us guiltless. Not to speak is to speak.
Not to act is to act." (Dietrich Bonhoeffer)

"Come here, boys." Dad called us over to where he sat when we were 7. "I want to show you something. Sit down." He patted the couch on either side of him. "It's time for you to see this."

"What?" Paul and I chorused.

Dad opened a thick scrapbook to the first page. A man in a flyer's uniform smiled up at us.

"Of course, you know this is your Uncle Robert." Dad laid one hand on my knee. "You're named for him. He won the Distinguished Flying Cross as a pilot in World War II."

Ten Words

"Cool," Paul said. "What did he fly?"

"B-17, a four-engine bomber. He flew with the 8th Air Force, based in England."

"Why did he fly?" I asked.

"There was a terrible war across the ocean, in Europe. A very bad man named Hitler, who wanted to rule the whole world, killed thousands and thousands of our people."

"Our people?"

"Yes, Jews, like us."

"Did our family die, too?"

"Distant cousins, yes."

Dad turned the page. Our eyes fell on another newspaper clipping. The photo showed emaciated bodies stacked like cordwood. Vacant eyes seemed to stare at us.

Paul and I drew back in horror.

Dad flipped another page. This photo showed a huge trench, ringed with soldiers and machine guns. In it lay the bodies of many, many dead people, arms and legs sticking up like broken tree branches.

"You may be young," Dad said, "but listen to me very, very carefully." He tapped the photos with a finger. "This is what happens when good people fail to act on their own goodness. This is what happens when good people remain silent. Sons …" He put an arm around each of us. "Always have the courage to challenge evil. Always."

❧❧❧

Declare it Fearlessly

"From my mother's womb
you have been my God." (Psalm 22:10)

"The word of the LORD came to me saying,
'Before I formed you in the womb, I knew you,
before you were born I set you apart.'" (Jeremiah 1:4-5)

Paul and I attended Temple Beth el in Niagara Falls, New York, for our religious education, while Dad taught us how to recognize social injustice at home. We watched the evening news as a family and paid special attention to the Civil Rights Movement.

"Hope is always based on a refusal to give up. It's a kind of saying to oneself, 'I'm going on in spite of.' It's what the existential philosophers would call 'the courage to be.' And if you have that, you can move on." Dad read from Martin Luther King's "Meaning of Hope" speech, delivered on March 15, 1968, at Central United Methodist Church in Detroit.

"You boys keep his words in your heart. He is a wise man."

Three weeks later, an assassin snuffed out Martin Luther King's earthly life.

"The world has lost a great man." Dad's voice shook. "A very great man."

"You need to meet Charlie," Paul told me when we were 15. "You've never talked to anybody like this kid. He's different."

"How?"

Ten Words

"He talks about God like they're best friends."

"I'd like to meet him," I said.

I met Charlie a few days later. *Paul was right. Charlie talks about God like he really knows him — as an intimate friend.*

"You can't talk about God like that," I told him. I had this vague idea that God sat, like an angry ogre, on a cloud, hefting a baseball bat, eager to bat me straight into hell the moment I messed up.

"I can't help it. God is my friend."

"How is that possible?" I asked. "I want to know God like that."

"Can we go to your church?" Paul asked.

"Of course."

Paul and I had never been in a gentile church. I expected some cold stone building from medieval Europe, but Charlie took us to a small country Methodist church.

Dad had raised us in the Jewish culture without introducing us to the God of our fathers. We observed Jewish holidays, such as Passover, from a cultural standpoint, void of any spiritual dimension.

The pastor spoke with genuine warmth and friendliness as he gave a message and prayed with the people. *Something greater than I've ever known is in this room.* Paul and I felt the lack of spirituality in our home but had no clue what it was or how to fix it. *Whatever these Christians possess, it's real.*

"We want to come back," we told Charlie after the service.

Declare it Fearlessly

"How about coming to New Life Mission this Friday? It's over at Emmanuel Methodist Church."

"Sure will."

Dr. Boldt, an evangelist from Plymouth, England, spoke that night. He laid out the Gospel of Jesus in clear terms and after his message, invited anyone present to go forward after the service who would like to meet Jesus.

Paul and I moved to the front as one.

"Jesus, I willingly confess my sins to you. I have not lived as I should. I have not obeyed as I ought. I realize my helplessness before you and ask you to come into my life. I yield my whole being to you as Lord and Savior. Please fill me with your Holy Spirit."

"Guess what?" we announced when we got home. "We became followers of Jesus tonight!"

"How could you do this?" Dad shouted. "How could you reject your heritage — reject *me*, your own father?"

His family had warned him that if he married a gentile, eventually his children would end up the same.

"You have spit in my face!" he roared.

Paul and I escaped to our rooms, while Dad raged on. I pressed my back against the closed door.

Sometime before this, a Catholic laywoman had given Paul and me a book to read, *Young Lions of Judah.* It recorded the testimonies of young Jewish males who sacrificed a great deal to follow Jesus. They had experienced the same spiritual vacuum we felt in our home. And, like them, we didn't view our conversion as turning our backs on Judaism. After all, we knew Jesus was Jewish. To us, conversion fulfilled our heritage.

Some people cavalierly accept Jesus as Savior, merely seeking a ticket into heaven. Lordship is entirely different. In that moment I knew our decision would cost and cost dearly.

I saturated myself in the Bible. I knew I had to yield to Jesus as Lord to survive the sudden, intense conflict in our home. We loved our dad, but we also knew the words of Jesus.

"If anyone comes to me and does not hate his father and mother ... yes, even his own life — he cannot be my disciple." I understood the verse from Luke 14 to mean that if we put anyone or anything before Jesus, we are not true disciples.

Dad's rejection hurt. I read the prophecies in the Old Testament that predicted the rejection of Jesus, and the Gospels recorded the fulfillment of the same. Dad's wrath intimidated me, but the truth of Jesus gave me the power to stand firm.

I learned lordship, and I learned it fast.

"Look, Marjorie." My father rattled the Jewish newspaper in his hands. "The obituary says Jonathan Bauer died." He turned to me. "Isn't he your age? What happened?"

"He converted to Jesus."

Dad's eyes dropped back to the paper. "They sat shiva," he said, referring to the Jewish custom of declaring apostates dead.

Declare it Fearlessly

"He was thrown out of their house, and they burned everything he owned," Paul added.

"Here we go again. Prejudice and evil." Dad laid the paper down and sighed. "Marjorie, we may not like the decision our sons have made to follow Jesus, but we can't stand by and watch another boy suffer like this."

"Jonathan can live with us," Mom said. Jonathan's presence and the circumstances that brought him to us helped build a bridge back to our parents.

ॐॐॐ

"Cheap grace is the deadly enemy of our church.
We are fighting today for costly grace."
(Dietrich Bonhoeffer)

Paul and I joined a Bible study class led by our Latin teacher, Mr. Houser, who was also a part-time Baptist pastor. We met after school.

"I want to share something with you kids before we begin our lesson," he said. "I just got back from visiting the underground church of persecuted Christians in the Soviet Union. Some of those people have died for their faith. You know something?" He gazed into each pair of eyes. "Those people are praying for *you* kids. Yes, you. You want to know why?" He waggled his finger.

We remained silent.

"Because it's too easy to be a Christian in America. There's not enough cost."

Ten Words

His words slammed into me. Being a Christ follower is — and always has been — costly. *Will I continue to live all-out for God, or will I wimp out?*

After graduating high school and then Bible school, I took a position at Teen Challenge in Rochester, New York, which housed 17 recovering heroin addicts. Some had already decided to follow Christ, others had not.

The phone awakened me after I'd retired for the night. I groped for the receiver.

"Hello?"

"Hi, honey. This is Mom. Are you sitting down?"

"Actually, Mom, I'm lying down. I've been asleep for some time. Is everything okay?"

"Better than okay. I went with a neighbor to hear Dale Evans Rogers speak tonight. She told the story of her life — her marriages, her kids, her career and her faith."

"Sounds interesting, Mom."

I loved her soft laugh. "Did you know that she found Christ when *her* son took her to church?"

"Uh, no."

"Dale Evans gave an invitation at the end of her talk. I went forward and accepted Jesus as my Lord and Savior."

After Mom yielded to the Lordship of Jesus, her daughters and their husbands followed. Only Dad held out. But I knew in my heart of hearts that Dad would eventually yield to Jesus. I never panicked as the years passed because I had come to understand that God works over a lifetime. Time limits humans, but not God.

Declare it Fearlessly

Dad reached out to Jesus and asked to be baptized — four days before he died in his 80th year.

అపి అపి అపి

"The test of the morality of a society is what
it does for its children." (Dietrich Bonhoeffer)

In 1988, I discovered *el Basurero*, the city dump, while in Mexico City on a speaking tour. I saw hundreds of children sorting trash and serving as sex slaves to corrupt syndicates in the area. People flew in from all over the world to satisfy their twisted lust on these children.

I went to a local official's office to beg for clean drinking water for them.

"Are these kids taxpayers?" he asked.

"Of course not! They're only children, abandoned by their parents."

He waved a dismissive hand. "Then they are only ghosts to me."

"Lord," I prayed on the flight home, "what can I do for these helpless children?" I meditated on Proverbs 3:27: "Do not withhold good from those who deserve it, when it is in your power to act."

"What can I do to make a lasting impact?"

One day I watched a news story about a young man who had run a marathon for a little girl who needed a liver transplant. I looked at a map, noting where I lived, near

Ten Words

the Canada/U.S border, and where those kids in the garbage piles lived. I decided to walk from the Canada/U.S. border to Mexico. During the 2,000-mile trek, which we named Faithwalk, I was granted countless interviews for TV and newspapers, successfully spreading the word and raising funds for those precious souls.

My brother, Paul, called me during that time.

"I've something I have to show you when you get home," he said.

"What is it?" I asked when I'd returned to Buffalo.

"A couple from my church brought this to me." He drew out a tiny package and withdrew a towel. There, in his arms, lay a perfectly formed human fetus.

"What? How?"

"They thought the clinic they live next to was a regular doctor's office. One night they checked the dumpster and found the remains of aborted babies. It's an abortion clinic."

Paul looked directly at me, his mirror image. "Rob, you've been raising money for kids who live in the dumps. Believe me, I applaud your work, but what are we going to do about the kids left *in* the dumpsters?"

I stared at the tiny, perfectly formed, dead human form and then at my brother.

"I'm going to hold a public funeral for all the remains we've recovered," Paul said.

Declare it Fearlessly

Paul and I began conducting street evangelism in front of abortion clinics in Buffalo, New York, our home city, where we passed out Christian literature and Bibles and offered help to desperate young mothers.

Not appreciating our presence, a group of clinic owners banded together in 1990 and found a judge willing to sign an order to stop our outreach. His order banned pro-lifers from offering literature, Bibles or prayer to those who claimed they were going to or coming from these clinics.

"Sidewalks are public property," Paul said. "To rule we can't distribute to anybody violates our First Amendment Rights."

"I agree. Anybody could claim to be going to the clinic, even these people going into the post office here. It would be their word against ours."

"Remember that story Dad told us when we were kids," Paul said, "the one about the fire on the Navy ship during World War II?"

"How could I forget? He repeated it often enough!"

"When the first officer approached the captain with the news, 'Sir, there's a fire in the engine room,' the captain never even looked at him. 'Put it out,' he told the officer."

"Don't get excited, just get the job done."

"Exactly. Dad raised us to challenge evil, and what that judge ordered is wrong."

"We won't stop our ministry."

Paul raised an eyebrow. "We'll get arrested."

Ten Words

"You're right. But that will give us the opportunity to bring our case before a judge."

We were reported, arrested and got our desire. We stood before the same judge who made the original ruling.

After representing ourselves and losing, we filed in a higher court.

The case crawled through the judicial system, finally reaching the U.S. Supreme Court in 1996.

Seven years after the original incident, we scored a mixed victory. The justices decided eight to one that the worst part of the court order was unconstitutional, but that some restrictions would remain. Still, it meant Christians could return to the sidewalks of America and share the love of God in Christ with those in crisis. That was victory enough!

చాచాచా

"We must be ready to allow ourselves to be interrupted by God." (Dietrich Bonhoeffer)

In 1993, while on a pro-life speaking tour in Florida's panhandle, a friend suggested I visit Abundant Life Church in nearby Fort Walton Beach with him. I accepted his invitation.

Shortly after the pastor, Bishop L.M. Thorne, began delivering his message, he paused.

"I have a word from the Lord for someone in this room."

He looked around and pointed at me, sitting in the second row. "Sir, could you stand, please?"

I complied.

"God wants to tell you he is planning to use you in extraordinary ways. He will bring you before leaders of nations."

I sat down — stunned.

My brother, Paul, had already told me he was considering an offer to pastor a small church in Washington, D.C. I'd felt an urge to move there as well.

I sat in my motel room several hours later, still chewing over the man's words to me. *Either someone tipped him off or he heard from God. That's impossible. Only my family knows of my thoughts. This is — this has to be of God. He is confirming what I've been feeling in my heart. Okay, Lord. I'm ready to follow you to D.C.*

After my decision to move, Paul got an offer from the American Center of Law and Justice, based in Virginia Beach, Virginia, to serve as the executive vice president.

"What am I going to do?" he asked me. "I've already committed to pastoring this church, but I feel God wants me at ACLJ."

"I can take the church."

We went before our denominational board with Paul's dilemma.

"You're identical twins," the leader said, smiling. "We'll take either one." So, in 1994, Paul went to Virginia Beach, while my wife, Cheryl, and I moved to D.C. with our two children to begin pastoring the church.

Ten Words

I began researching the spiritual climate of Washington, D.C. I learned about Christian groups who focus on the White House, and others on the Congress, but nowhere could I find anyone ministering on behalf of the federal judicial system.

God began moving my heart to pray for these justices. Dad had taught his sons well — when you see a need, you meet it.

In 1996, while attending a reception held for members of Congress, my pager beeped. I recognized the phone number as belonging to a member of my growing church. I excused myself to take the call.

"We're at the emergency room," the caller told me. "We've been in a terrible car accident."

My heart felt torn. I knew God was using me at the reception, touching the lives of people not easily reached, but I also knew my church people needed me at that very moment. I drove to the emergency room.

It's time to move on. God spoke into my heart. *I have another job for you now.*

I went back to the board. "I feel God wants me to minister fulltime to our federal judges," I said. "I can't do both jobs well."

"We'll release you as soon as you find a replacement for your church."

I went home and called my friend Mark Batterson. "How would you like to take over my pastorate at National Community Church?"

"I don't even have to pray about it. My wife and I knew

God moved us to Washington for a reason, we just didn't know what it was at the time. Now I do." Mark laughed. "Yes, I'll take it."

I founded Faith and Action in 1995 as a Christian missionary outreach to top-level government officials in Washington, D.C. Our purpose is to affect the hearts and minds of America's public policymakers with the mandate given by Christ in the two greatest Commandments: Love God with all your heart, soul, mind and strength; and love your neighbor as yourself.

Through our Ten Commandments Project, we give plaques of the same to members of Congress and other officials in high positions. Both Presidents Bill Clinton and George W. Bush have accepted our plaques.

Over the years, Faith and Action has developed four pillars for truth, events held every year at the nation's capital:

First Pillar: Annual National Conference for the Pre-born and Their Mothers and Fathers

This is the only pro-life service of its kind to be held within the U.S. Capitol Complex. We hold this conference each year on the anniversary of the Roe vs. Wade Supreme Court decision, which legalized abortion on demand in America. We always leave the doors wide open so passersby can hear the prayers and preaching. It's not uncommon to see a member of Congress hesitate at the door, move on, then return, move on again and finally stop and peer in. Many of these legislators bring up the topic of the conference during the year.

Second Pillar: U.S. Capitol Bible Reading Marathon

For four days and nights, members of Congress, civic and religious leaders and people of faith from all over America come to read the Bible aloud on the west steps of the U.S. Capitol, where our presidents are sworn into office. Microphones echo the word of God down the National Mall as readers begin at Genesis, chapter 1, and continue, without commentary, to the last chapter of Revelation.

We love to watch the windows facing the steps. On the first day, many crack open, just a smidge. On day two, they open wider. By the fourth day, we can see the movers and shakers of our nation with their ears plastered against their wide-open windows. This event ends with the onset of the third pillar.

Third Pillar: National Day of Prayer at U.S. Supreme Court

This is the *only* public prayer service held on the grounds of the U.S. Supreme Court. A few years ago, if a person simply bowed his head in silent prayer he would be arrested and charged with illegal activity within the Capitol Complex. Faith and Action approached the

Supreme Court and said, "You are the keepers of the Constitution, and you are breaking the law of the land by arresting people who pray on these grounds. We can go public with this violation of our First Amendment Rights, or we can settle it quietly."

The Supreme Court settled. Prayer returned to the complex. Now, on the National Day of Prayer, pastors gather with Faith and Action to pray for each justice by name. We ask that God's grace and wisdom guide them in their deliberations and the decisions they make.

Fourth Pillar: The Live Nativity at U.S. Supreme Court

Every November, Faith and Action stages the only live nativity scene procession in which the participants walk from our office to the front of the U.S. Supreme Court. There we hold a brief ceremony and return. We do this for two reasons. First, we want to publicly bear witness on Capitol Hill to the truth that Christmas is the celebration of the incarnation of Jesus Christ — God becoming flesh and dwelling among us. Second, Operation Nativity serves to remind people of faith across our nation that if we can stage a crèche, or nativity scene, in front of the highest court in the land, they have the right to stage nativities in front of public buildings in their own communities.

ॐ ॐ ॐ

Ten Words

"'Well done, my good servant!' his master replied.
'Because you have been trustworthy
in a very small matter, take charge of 10 cities.'"
(Luke 19:17, God's Word Bible)

"I'd like you to meet someone," a friend said when I visited Christ the Redeemer Church, Centreville, Virginia, in 2008.

We shook hands.

"What do you do?" I asked.

"I'm a federal judge."

I covered my surprise. One doesn't meet federal judges every day and certainly not Christian ones. He'd given his occupation as casually as he would a comment about the weather.

We talked about the challenge of living as a disciple of Jesus in the federal system.

"Say," he said, "the federal judges have a breakfast meeting once a month. Why don't you come and be our speaker sometime?"

"Me? I've never done such a venue before, but, yes, I'd be honored."

"I'll give you a call."

Several months passed. Then he called. "You going to be in town next week?"

"Yes, Judge. Why do you ask?"

"Remember when we talked about the breakfast meeting with the justices? We'd like you to be our speaker at the next one."

"Thank you. I'm pleased you remembered and asked me, but what should I speak on?"

"How about that book you wrote, about the meaning of the Ten Commandments?"

"Sure."

"Remember," he warned me, "no Bible thumping. This isn't a revival meeting."

"But the Ten Commandments addresses quite clearly man's situation, that we've all sinned, and God's expectations of us, that we all need to repent, and the solution he provides in his son, Jesus. If I talk like that, I'm going to have to issue an invitation at the end."

"Well, we can pray on that." I felt his nerves over the phone. "Let me call you back."

A few minutes later, the phone rang.

"Let's do it," he said.

"Good morning." The judge stood up to introduce me. His hands seemed to tremble as he smoothed out the page on which was written my formal introduction.

"It's my distinct honor to introduce to you Reverend Rob Schenck, whom I think you will find very interesting. He's written a book about the Ten Commandments, and he's here to explain their importance and relevance in our society." He fidgeted with his hands. "And he's been arrested several times."

Are you joking? Mortification heated my face. *What will these people think?* I stood up and stumbled to the podium. Every eye in the room focused on me, and most faces seemed to say, *Go ahead. We dare you to explain yourself.*

I faced my audience and took a long, deep, slow breath. I glanced down at a copy of my book, *The Ten Words That Will Change a Nation*, and recalled the instructions I felt God had given me. *Use these words to bring the Gospel to these people.*

"The Ten Commandments are revered by Judaism, Christianity and Islam. Whether we like it or not, they rest deep in American culture, in our nation's spiritual DNA."

I held up an image of the twin stones on which God wrote the Ten Commandments to his people, knowing that the moment each justice laid eyes on it, he or she would face the reality of sin versus righteousness. I explained the true Hebraic meaning of each of the 10 words.

"These words reveal humanity's condition from God's perspective rather than our own. Whether we like it or not, we are triune beings of spirit, soul and body. When we ignore our spiritual selves, we live in only two dimensions of our being, like a flat plane. This causes a vague dissatisfaction of life and restlessness in our soul because we are unaware of or ignoring that dimension that gives us texture and meaning in life — the spiritual dimension.

"We remain unfulfilled until we recognize there is a reality beyond the body and mind — the reality of God, his laws, his demands and his willingness to partner with humanity.

Declare it Fearlessly

"The Ten Words are a moral compass to point the human spirit into an understanding of true right and real wrong. Only then can we see the depth of God's holiness against our sinfulness and realize our need of a Savior to bridge the gap between us and him."

I finished my speech. Most of the justices seemed to show a mild interest. "Now that I've explained to you the claims of Christ …" I looked down at my audience, and suddenly I remembered the homework I'd done, reading up on the justices present and their religious histories.

"Ladies and gentlemen of the bench, I respect your service as men and women of the law." I folded my notes and stashed them in a pocket. "I want to ask you a question. I want you to go back in time, to your childhood, and think about your own personal history.

"I know my audience today. I studied the percentages of Lutheran and Catholic, Presbyterian and Episcopalian and even some Jewish, like myself, in this room. Many of you were baptized into your respective churches as infants, and promises were made on your behalf, by your parents, your godparents and even by the entire congregation at that event. I've read the vows of the various churches, and they are beautiful ones. Promises that were made vicariously for you because you were too young to make them yourselves.

"So, my question to you is this: How many of you sitting here today have made those same vows from your own heart to God's heart? Please take a moment to think about this. How many of you here today are ready to make this promise for yourselves? How many here are willing to promise, before God, that you will yield to his claim on your life and make Christ your Lord, Master and Savior?

"I am an Evangelical Christian, and we have a little ritual of raising one's hand to indicate one's commitment. Could you please join me in this ritual?"

I scanned the room. Not one hand rose.

They're going to roast that judge for inviting me here. My eyes locked on the EXIT sign. *I just want to get out of here in one piece.*

Then I saw one hand poke up about halfway, retreat, go back up a little farther, retreat again and finally go all the way up. This time the hand held. One after another, more hands joined the first, all over the room.

I counted 14 hands. *This is fantastic.* A woman began weeping and boldness crept into my heart.

"Thank you. I've seen your hands. But, more importantly, God saw them. Now, I'd like to invite those who raised their hands to come up here so I can pray for each one of you."

Altogether, 28 federal justices — twice as many as raised their hands — came to the front. I glanced over at my host. His eyes popped.

I smiled. *What a beautiful end to this meeting.* My heart rejoiced in another proof of God's goodness and faithfulness.

Later that day, my office hired bike couriers to deliver Bibles and literature to all those who'd come up for prayer.

God had indeed done his greatest work through me

when I felt the weakest. That one event proved the turning point for my accessibility to federal judges. True friendships take years to form on Capitol Hill because each justice, every member of Congress, even the president, wants to know what I really want to gain from an alliance. What's my true angle? My true motive?

After that meeting, justices realized my genuine desire to serve them, and they began opening their hearts to me. On June 7, 2010, the board and membership of the Capitol Hill Executive Service Club appointed me as their chaplain.

I continue to work through Faith and Action, while my "former womb-mate," Paul, serves as the director of our companion organization, the National Pro-Life Center on Capitol Hill, which is located just one door from ours in this block of historic contiguous row houses.

❧❧❧

"So how can I find your office?" a caller asks.

"Just look for the Ten Commandments sculpture on Capitol Hill, right behind the Supreme Court. You can't miss them," I say, referring to the 850-pound granite stones, measuring 3 feet by 3 feet. "When you find them, you've found us."

Ten words that *will* change our nation.

Whatever the Cost
The Story of
Pastor Steven Ddamulira Mayanja
Written by Alexine Garcia

"I am tired of the witchcraft. I am tired of this darkness we live in," I told my cousin. "I can no longer take this death and violence everywhere, but this is the path our family has chosen for us. What other choice do we have?"

My cousin and I were chosen by our family to become the next priests and to inherit the family gods. We were destined to practice witchcraft for the rest of our lives. Witch doctors were revered in Uganda and often sought out, but my cousin and I understood the dark depression that came with this calling.

"Suicide is our best option," he responded grimly.

"I agree, but then what?" I asked. Neither of us had an answer. "Why don't we look for the born-agains?" Even as I said it, hope rose inside of me.

కొకొకొ

A few days later, I walked around the city capital looking for a job. I also hoped I would find these born-again believers. They were not easy to find, considering the political climate of Uganda at that time. The Ugandan

Declare it Fearlessly

President, Idi Amin, had declared Uganda a Muslim state and closed down all the churches. He wanted all the young people to grow up as Muslims. But it wasn't just the Muslim beliefs that consumed our city.

Witchcraft was practiced every place you turned. Families collected pictures of their ancestors, statues, tiny relics and anything they could find to place their trust in. I didn't know it back then, but I came to be convinced that in each of those gods and relics resided a demon force bringing a dark oppression into our lives. I believe those same spirits whispered ideas of suicide into our ears.

But something greater began working in my life — the Holy Spirit. I decided to visit another cousin in town after I couldn't find a job, much less the believers. I sat outside my family's house feeling defeated. I came to this place to look for something better, and I was about to leave empty. Then a stranger, George O'Mio, sat beside me and introduced himself. He began telling me about Jesus. As I listened, I said to myself, *This is the kind of person I was looking for.* His words filled me with hope.

"Jesus came to set the captives free. Jesus said, 'All you who are heavy laden, come to me, and I will give you rest.'"

That is what I want, my soul said inside of me. When he asked if I wanted to accept Christ, I immediately said yes. "I've got my answer now; it is my time to cross over to the other side of hope."

And so on that last day of 1977, I became free for the first time. I received the Holy Spirit, and I spoke in tongues with such joy. George took me to the underground church to meet other believers. They met and worshipped in each other's homes to hide from the government persecution.

That same day when I got home, I went straight to my altar of inherited gods. I took the photos, the evil statues, jewelry, relics and everything else to the yard and lit them all on fire.

"What are you doing? Have you gone mad?" my mother screamed, clutching her chest. Everybody thought that I was going crazy. But I smiled and felt overwhelming joy fill every inch of me as the smoke of dying demons rose into the sky.

Our president was overthrown in 1979, and his Muslim power was lifted. Release from his rule came with the grave price of war and death. Soldiers killed for no good reason in every corner of Uganda. They had authority to murder with little to no consequence.

Despite the violence, the underground churches were opened to the public, and we worshipped without hiding. I served as an usher and sang in the choir at my own church.

I also had been accepted into a technical school and was learning to be an auto mechanic. I had graduated in 1980 during a strong economic crisis in Uganda, and it was very difficult to find a job. Finally, several years later in 1983, I found work as an auto mechanic.

Although the Muslim rule was lifted, great oppression, poverty and violence surrounded us. My cousin, Fred, and his wife, Parusi, were killed in their own home. I received the call only a few days after starting my job.

I arrived upon a scene of chaos and horror. The expressions on their faces showed that they lost their lives begging for mercy. Their three children roamed the house crying and in shock. Moses was 5 years old, Sylia was 3 and the baby, Chelsea, only 9 months. Fred had family in the United States, and so the news spread quickly to the States. His cousin, Gladys Lukyamuzi, attended Seattle Bible College in Washington. Her friends Roger and Cheryl Tornga in Washington State offered to adopt the three orphans. They even felt called by God to visit Uganda and pick the children up. This happened during a time of great political unrest in which no one was willing to visit our country.

However, this faithful couple showed up in March of 1983. Getting all the documents approved was an overwhelming burden. Birth certificates and passports caused so much trouble for us. On top of that, many of our family members opposed this couple adopting the children. However, their grandmother knew that there was no hope here in Uganda for these children.

On the day before the passports were scheduled to be signed, the government official in charge of the task was killed. Our hopes sank into the ground, and Roger and Cheryl had no choice but to return home and postpone the adoption.

As we waited for Roger's plane to arrive, he made the mistake of snapping a photo of me at the airport. Police immediately surrounded us. We found ourselves in prison for a simple photo, charged with espionage.

I thank God that Roger had the opportunity to speak with the police. "I enjoyed Uganda. I don't want to go home with a bad memory. Can you please take the film, and let us go?" Roger and I were released from jail, and we returned to the airport. As we awaited his departure, he looked into my eyes and began to cry.

"Why are you crying, my friend?"

"Steve, God wants you to go to Bible college."

I chuckled at the very idea and shook my head. "No, I am a mechanic. I just sing in the choir. And I am a simple usher. I don't think Bible college is for me."

"God just spoke to me. I have to give you a ticket to America to attend Bible college where my wife attended. Seattle Bible College."

"No, this is some kind of mistake."

"God is waiting for you, Steve. Take my business card. One day God will speak to you. When he does, you write to me, and let me know." In my heart, I felt that Roger was mistaken.

I went back to my job as a mechanic and continued to serve at church. In January 1985, the company I worked for gave me a bicycle with a small gasoline engine attached. It was so unique that every time I traveled, people in my village were intrigued. The kids surrounded me, calling, "Born-again man, we want to see your bicycle." I showed it to them and let a few of them ride it.

We laughed and had a good time, and they all started to leave. As they walked away, the Lord rebuked me and said, *Is that all you can offer to my children?* So I called them back and talked to them about Jesus. We sang, and I gave them candy.

"We love your house, born-again man! Can we come every day?"

"No, you just come on Sunday afternoon," I said half-heartedly. The honest truth was that I didn't expect much of it.

The following Sunday on my way home from church, I found about 30 kids waiting for me on the road. Twenty more waited at my house.

"We brought all of our friends," one child said, so excited. On that day, God changed my ministry from just singing in the choir to ministering to children. As I looked at this crowd of smiling faces in front of me, I had no clue what to teach them. I came up with a Bible story and sang songs with them. Little by little, I bought benches and Bibles with pictures. That is how I started a church for the children. Then I visited the schools and ministered to kids there.

I prayed and fasted to grow closer to the Lord. One day while at work in my small office, I read the Bible while my co-workers ate lunch. The Spirit of God came over me and told me it was time to go to Bible college. I quickly found some paper and a pen and wrote a letter to Roger to let him know that God had finally spoken to me, two years later.

Whatever the Cost

In October 1986, I moved to the United States and attended Seattle Bible College. I soaked up everything I learned. Then in my second year, I found myself in another moment of intense prayer and fasting in which I felt that God spoke to me so clearly.

Go back to your village, and open a church.

My first instinct was to object.

I am not even done with Bible college, Lord. This was of no concern to God, and the urging did not leave. He even told me the name of the ministries that I would start: Uganda Christian Outreach Ministries.

While deep in prayer, I received a vision of a tall white man. In this dream, he traveled with me to Uganda. *Take this man to your village. He will help you to start my ministry in your village.*

I walked around my college looking for this man, but he was nowhere to be found.

I did not give up because I knew that God had given this promise.

"Steven, would you like to come with some classmates to my church?" a classmate asked.

I loved to visit American churches. "Yes, of course. How could I say no to such an offer?"

After the service, we spent time in fellowship with other believers in the lobby. Right then I saw the very man God showed me in my dream. I immediately went up to him.

"Hello, sir, my name is Steven. I am from Uganda."

Declare it Fearlessly

"Nice to meet you. My name is Ron Devore. What brings you to America?"

"I am attending Seattle Bible College. I am supposed to return home this June and start a church. This may sound crazy to you, but God showed me your face in a vision. You are meant to come with me to start a whole ministry."

The color left his face. "What? No! You are very mistaken," he said. "I cannot leave the United States, and I don't do Africa. I am going to France in June, actually." He walked away, seeming to be in a state of shock. Despite his unfavorable reaction, I didn't worry. I knew what God showed me, and I knew it would come to pass.

ॐॐॐ

I was excited for a new class I planned to take on the book of the Acts of the Apostles. I read the book and really enjoyed learning how God used these people to launch churches. I decided to talk to the professor about my endeavor.

"Hello, Professor. I wondered if you could give me some advice."

"Sure, what can I help you with?"

I handed him a notepad and a pen and asked him, "God has called me to return to Uganda and start a ministry. Can you please give me some tips that I will need to know about starting a new church?"

"Wow, you're really serious about this, aren't you?"

"Yes. God has told me to return to my village in June."

Whatever the Cost

"Well, I really like your zeal. I think this is something my church could take part in. I am going to talk to the leadership at my church, and I will get back with you."

Only a few days later, my professor took me to his church to meet with a specific elder and his wife that he knew would be interested in this church planting. I chuckled to myself as he began to introduce me to the very man God had shown me in my dream.

"Yes, I have met Steve," Ron said with a grin. This was all it took for Ron and his wife, Shirley, to accept that it was truly God's will for them to travel to Africa.

In June of 1987, we arrived in Uganda and got right to work. All the children in the village and surrounding schools were familiar with me from our Bible studies. Word flew through the village that I was bringing an American, and the excitement buzzed. We rented a disco hall and held our first church service on June 21. That day Ron preached in English while I translated, and more than 100 people accepted the Lord during two different services. Ron began teaching two-month discipleship classes Monday through Friday. It was a sight to see the classroom fill up with eager hearts. Each day the students grew in their relationship with Christ.

After two months of the ministry going strong, I felt God's call to return to Seattle Bible College. I didn't understand why he called me back and now wanted me to return to the States, but I obeyed his call. Before I left, we placed Steven Kawesa, a close friend of mine, in the head pastor role. On top of that, we were blessed with an offer to buy land. We purchased 5 acres for around $450. To this day, the base of our ministry is on this land.

I finished my degree in 1989, and once again, God began calling me home. I made so many excuses to stay in the comfort of America, but there was really no way my heart could disobey. I became an ordained pastor and returned with my friends Ron and Shirley to continue in the ministry.

Many American churches came together to donate a container full of all kinds of items for our ministry. We received furniture, medical supplies, equipment, clothes and even a large truck. When I went home, the work carried on. Our group planted churches, preached the Gospel and ministered to those who needed the love of Christ.

When we arrived in Uganda with our container, we went straight to the Revenue Authority to get a tax exemption for our donations. We were late, and the office was about to close, so we had to run up the stairs to the third floor. As we rushed to meet a government official, a beautiful lady was coming down the steps, and I could not help myself. I stared.

"Wow, praise the Lord!" The words escaped my lips before I could think.

"Amen," she responded with a smile.

Sitting in the Revenue Office filling out paperwork, I could not stop thinking about this beautiful woman. As we walked down the same flight of stairs, I prayed to God, *Lord, when will I see her again?*

Whatever the Cost

God answered my prayer immediately. She stood talking with our driver as we came out of the building.

"Steve and Ron, meet Cissy," the driver said. "When you first opened the church, she was one of those who got saved after we left."

That very day I knew I would marry that woman. She attended one of the Jesus Loves You churches, called Segduku Worship Center, and we married a year later.

The large truck that came in the container was a big Nissan pickup, and it played an important role in our ministry. Everywhere we drove it, people pointed and looked at us with amazement. I knew that somehow we had to use this truck to bring attention to God and not ourselves. I prayed and asked God, *Lord, how can we use this pickup to bring you glory?* God answered and instructed me to write big words on the truck for everyone to see. We wrote in our language: "Are you born again? Jesus Loves You!" And so, people called us the Jesus Loves You church. The name became so popular that we adopted it as our official slogan. We passed a resolution to name all of our projects Jesus Loves You, or Yesu Akwagala. Those same words were also painted on every vehicle we owned.

అఅఅ

In the early '90s, Pastor Ron and Shirley took a crusade to Musaka in Southern Uganda, a small village with no electricity or any utilities.

Declare it Fearlessly

"Jesus came to set the captives free," Ron told the crowd day after day. Each time he spoke, people rose from their chairs and came to the altar to experience a life change.

Ron and Shirley stayed in a small tent during their time in this village. The air was hot and humid, and a layer of sweat drenched every piece of clothing. One day, Ron noticed a small girl named Night. He found it peculiar that she was not in school in the middle of the day. As he sat watching her play, the Holy Spirit spoke to him so clearly: *Help my child.*

Ron immediately answered, "Lord, we don't have money for this sort of thing. We are stretched thin, and this is not good timing."

The Holy Spirit persisted: *Feed my child.* He went inside his tent and left the girl outside playing in the dirt.

A few days later, Ron was returning to his tent when he ran into Night again. He decided to stop and talk to her through a translator.

"My mother and father are dead," emerged from her tiny lips.

Ron was moved with compassion for this little girl, but deep inside his answer was still no. He just could not conceive of how the ministry could possibly care for this girl. He gave her a bottle of Coke and returned to his tent. When he stepped out moments later, he stopped still at the sight before him. A line of six girls sat on a bench. Night placed a straw inside the Coke bottle and gave each girl a sip of her soda before taking her own first sip. This was the very first soda she ever drank, yet she shared it with all her friends. God spoke to his heart: *If she can share like this, why can't you share what little I have given you?*

As with any other crusade, the time came to go home. When Ron arrived back at his trailer, he was greeted by a fax from his son-in-law, Rob Holiday.

Papa Ron,

God spoke to me to encourage the families in our church to start sponsoring children in Africa. He even gave me a name to call this program: Feed My Lambs. Can you please look for orphans, and I will continue to look for money here.

God bless,
Rob Holiday

To this day, thousands of children have been sponsored and have turned their lives around. Some of them are now lawyers or professionals or ministry workers in our program.

As the program grew, we began to realize we didn't have the resources to care for newborns through 4 year olds. It was not an issue for God, though. A young woman named Bethany visited our ministry during her summer break from school. Her parents were pastors in California, and she had a deep love for the Lord. One day, she sat listening intently as Ron spoke of the need and desire to build a babies' home right on our property.

"We can build a home for the babies who are abandoned in toilets and trashcans throughout Uganda. People can bring us these babies, and we will raise them learning about the Lord. We don't have the funds or the means now, but this is something that God will surely provide for."

What Ron did not know was that Bethany had always had a desire in her heart to open an orphanage. She knew this was a calling on her life, but she didn't know where God would lead her to open this facility. Hearing Ron speak set her heart on fire with an answer from the Holy Spirit. Back in California, Bethany went right to work raising the needed funds. In 1995, we opened Bethany's Children's Home. The babies that came into the home were often sitting on the edge of the grave. It was a miracle to watch a resurrection take place in their lives. We continue to witness the hand of God give these precious children a second chance.

Abandoned babies are a common occurrence here in our nation. The police often bring babies who have been found in dumpsters or public restrooms to our orphanage. It was such a miracle to us when one of these very babies landed right in our own home.

We were a family with three boys and one girl. For the longest time my wife yearned for another little girl. Her conviction came from a promise that God gave her. He blessed her with such an assurance that she would indeed receive another girl. However, it was a matter of waiting, and that was not something my wife was fond of. We couldn't visit the Bethany home without her nearly adopting a child. One evening she sat straight up in bed and spoke to me. "Don't you think it's time for us to get our baby girl? Why don't we go over to the orphanage and adopt a girl?"

"No, Cissy, God will bring us a girl in his timing."

A few weeks later, our neighbor Ruth encountered a desperate woman ready to abandon her baby. The woman had just stepped off a bus, and as Ruth laid eyes on her, she saw a weak, tired expression on her face. The baby in her arms looked frail and dirty.

"Are you okay? You look like you have just given birth."

"I did just give birth."

Ruth looked down at the baby and saw that it was not even cleaned from the delivery.

"We need to take care of this baby. Why don't you come home with me?" The two went to Ruth's house and gave the baby a bath. The woman looked bewildered and shared her despair with Ruth.

"I don't want this baby. I tried to have an abortion three times, and it just wouldn't work. I made the choice to kill this baby when it was born. But when I was about to do it, a strong fear came over me. This girl is dangerous, and I don't want her."

Ruth looked at the woman and had no idea what to say.

"I will be back; I need to get some air," the woman told her. But she didn't return.

Ruth's husband was not happy with this news. The family struggled to provide for their own children. Their finances were just not enough to take on another baby. Ruth continued to care for the baby for the next month while they decided what to do. She really had no choice but to take the baby to the police.

"I am going to church, and then I will take the baby," she told her husband.

That Sunday morning, I was teaching from the book of Esther. I spoke of how Esther was an orphan with no mother or father. But Mordecai raised her in the ways of God, and he found himself in the palace as a great leader because of her. "You never know what could happen when you give an orphan a chance. God can use that child to take you to your destiny."

Ruth was so touched that she went home to rethink what she would do.

That week an associate and I walked through the village ministering to our neighbors when we approached Ruth's house. We were very surprised to hear a baby crying in her house.

"You have a baby, Ruth?" I asked her.

"She is not mine."

"What is her name?"

"She has no name. I was going to take her to the police. A woman abandoned her at my house. But I heard your message the other day, and I couldn't just leave her."

Whatever the Cost

"You should call her Queen Esther, then." We laid our hands on this precious child.

A few days later the mother came back to check on the baby, and Ruth tried to give her back. When she did, the woman became hysterical. She grabbed the baby in her arms and left, walking down the road right at dusk, crying and wailing. She walked for quite a while, and it became dark. She then came to a crowd of men who were alarmed at her behavior.

"What is wrong with you, ma'am? Why are you crying?" one man asked her.

"I want to die, I am tired of life. The problem I have is this baby."

The men were moved for her, and one man pulled a wad of money from his wallet. "Do not take your life. Take this money instead; it will help with caring for your baby."

"I don't even want your money. I just want to die."

"What you need is prayer," another man said to her. "Go up to that church at the top of the hill, and the pastor will help you."

She arrived at our front door around 9 p.m. My wife brought her into the house and talked to her. A little while later, she came into my office. "You need to come talk to this woman." As I laid eyes on her, my first reaction was shock. She had a crazy look in her eye, her hair was wild and uncombed and there was an expression of sheer desperation all over her face. Then I saw Queen Esther sprawled in her arms.

"That is the baby from Ruth's house."

"Yes, it is. She says she cannot care for it. She doesn't want it. I don't want it. I don't know what to do."

My wife looked at the baby as her heart filled with hope and empathy for this tiny baby. "We will help take this burden from you. The first thing we need to do is go to the police."

"I'm not going to the police! You just want to have me locked up." I became alarmed as I watched the hysteria rise in her face, but my wife spoke in a soothing voice and calmed her down.

"No, you must understand if you want us to take this baby, we need to involve the authorities and do it right. We truly want to help you with this burden."

We went to the government officials, and the woman signed her baby over to them. They immediately handed the baby over to us. That was the day that God held true to his promise and gave us our second girl.

రెరెరెరె

The Muslim religion has been like a dark cloud over Uganda that only rains down fear and depression. Witch doctors practice everywhere in our country, often sought out for all kinds of ailments and troubles. People seldom see that these men are full of their own ailments and troubles which they only pass on to others through witchcraft. Becoming a witch doctor is something that is often passed on to a person at birth. They inherit all the gods a family has accumulated, just like my cousin and I were expected to do. These are not merely empty statues and relics. Within these items reside demons, I believe, which overpower and take control of people's lives. But God is stronger than anything the enemy can do in our country, and we have seen many souls released from witchcraft.

Our team once taught in a small community, and we planned to launch a church. I stood under a tent in front of a crowd of Africans and told them about God's call to rest. "Jesus wants to bless you. He says to you, 'All you who are heavy laden, come to me, and I will give you rest.'" We were not surprised to see so many people answer the offer of salvation. But we were rather shocked the next morning when a witch doctor visited our camp.

"Are you the man who preached last night?"

"Yes, I am. Is there something I can help you with?"

"I am in so much need. This community sees me like a snake, and people are out to kill me. I don't know what to do anymore, and I am so tired. I need help."

"What you need is Jesus. Jesus can give you the rest you need, and he can set you free from the darkness you live under." The man began to lose the awful scowl, and I watched hope fill his face as God spoke through me.

I prayed over him, and he received salvation and deliverance from all the oppression in his life.

"I am so grateful," he said with tears of joy. "I would like you to come to my house." That same day we visited this man's home, which was connected to a temple where members of the community and his family came to worship the evil spirits. We took his collection of gods that were dedicated to the spirits, piled them up and set a mighty fire. He donated his land and asked us to build a church for Jesus right on the property. To this day, Bakijululoa Worship Center is a place people can come and be set free.

In August of 2013, another witch doctor came to see us at a church service. He was dying of some unknown sickness. This man was going to be rushed to a hospital, but his son, a believer in Christ, brought him to our church. The witch doctor was a big man who appeared well-fed, but unhappiness and weakness lined his face. After the Gospel message and the invitation to receive the forgiveness of Christ was given, this man rose from his seat and walked to the altar. Members of the church prayed over him and cast out the demons residing alongside his soul.

I stood at the exit as the service ended, greeting each person. He came up to me with a mighty smile on his face and shook my hand.

"I would like you to come to my village. There are a few things I want to show you," he said.

We sent some of the graduates from our Bible college, and they preached the Gospel to his mother, wife, children and neighbors.

Every single one of them received salvation. The whole group celebrated with prayer, laughter and praise to God as they set the pile of demon gods on fire. A church dedicated to worshipping God went up in that community and is a beacon of light for everyone.

Moments like these excited me because I got to see the Spirit of God moving. There was just something so amazing about watching someone set free, just like God did for me more than 36 years prior. These people came to church or one of the crusades looking terrible. They arrived with a deep sadness written upon their souls, and we watched the transformation take over their face with a smile and brilliant light. Sometimes they cried tears of joy, but there is always some kind of expression. Truly a sight to see. For this very reason, we host crusades every month. This is our life purpose, and we remain dedicated to reaching the lost, whatever the cost.

These moments in our ministry constantly reminded me of the original Queen Esther and her bold statements as recorded in the Old Testament. She went to Mordecai and asked him to pray and fast with her. She told him, "I am going to face the king. If I perish, then I perish." This is the same attitude of our ministry. We know that even if there is a risk in the work we do, God will protect us. We do it all for his glory and not our own.

In 1996, we bought land in the Musaka District to expand our ministry. I had to conceal my beliefs because the Muslim leaders and witch doctors in this area had vowed to never sell land to a born-again believer. However, I was certain God wanted us there. After the church was built, two of our ministry workers visited a nearby prison to witness to the inmates. These prisoners were treated very badly. They lived in poor conditions and led miserable lives. The first day the two visited, 20 out of 21 inmates accepted Christ. The transformation in their lives was immediate and visible to everyone. The prison guards were so amazed to see the prisoners singing songs of praise and carrying on with joy. The main officer at the facility requested that I come and meet with him.

"We want to know what you did to these inmates. They are like completely different people now."

"Well, we showed them love, and we shared the truth of the Gospel of Jesus with them. They are now born again."

"We have spoken to the officer in charge of all the prisons in the whole district, and he would like you to do the same in all of our facilities. Is this possible?"

I sat in shock at how amazing God was. I knew he had us in this region for a reason. There was no doubt that he planned to do great things. I immediately called Pastor Ron, and we planned all the details of the new ministry. Our workers traveled from one prison to another on foot. We invested in bicycles, then soon realized we'd be better off changing to motorbikes. Then we realized the difficulty of preaching to a hungry crowd. Also, many inmates had health issues that went untreated. We raised money for food and medical supplies and started visiting the prisons throughout Uganda in vans. Watching a nationwide ministry grow from two servants ministering on bikes was indeed like watching a miracle.

Whatever the Cost

❧❧❧

Back during my time at Seattle Bible College, God spoke to me and told me that one day I would start a Bible college in Africa. God also gave the same vision to Ron. We knew that it was God's will for us to disciple Africans. In 1993, I asked an engineer friend to create the plans for the building, and I tucked them away in my desk. I knew that this would all happen in God's timing. I shared this vision that God put in my heart with many others, and they just couldn't reciprocate my zeal. A classmate of mine, Eddie Pohlreich, ministered with us and had a deep love for the Lord.

Many years later in 1998, I sat in my office studying when Eddie came pounding on my door.

"Come in."

"Steven! Have you seen a vision or perhaps an angel of the Lord?"

I chuckled at his excitement. "No, Eddie, I haven't, but I assume you have."

"You won't believe it. I saw a river flowing from the top of our land here at the church. This river flowed to the entire village, to all Uganda and to the entire continent! It even flowed to other continents. God spoke to me and told me this was the mighty river of a Bible college."

I smiled at him, and the peace of God truly working in his own timing filled my soul. I pulled out the plans and slid them across the desk.

"You already have plans?"

"Of course I do. God spoke to me 10 years ago about your vision."

"I'm going to take a trip to America to raise the money we need."

Today students come from all over Africa to attend Jesus Loves You Bible College.

We have graduated students from Burundi, Rwanda, Sudan, Tanzania, Kenya, Uganda and Somalia. God brings them from everywhere.

જેન્જેન્જ

Years ago, when I told Roger that I was merely a simple choir singer, it was fear that spoke. It was fear of the calling God had on my life that stopped me from leaving that very day on a plane to Seattle Bible College.

Then my pastor preached Jeremiah 1:5 and 1:10, which reads: "Before I formed you in the womb I knew you, before you were born I set you apart; I appointed you as a prophet to the nations ... See, today I appoint you over nations and kingdoms to uproot and tear down, to destroy and overthrow, to build and to plant." Those verses worked in my heart to wake me up and hear God's voice clearly.

Fear causes us to turn away from our calling and create hundreds of excuses not to do what God has created us for. You have to discover that God has called you and given you a gift of ministering.

Whatever the Cost

Jeremiah told God, "I am too young."

Moses said, "I stammer."

I told Roger, "I am a mechanic, and I sing. I don't do Bible college."

When God showed me Ron in my vision, Ron said, "I don't do Africa."

We will always have excuses when we disobey God. But God knows your number. God knew Jeremiah's number. He told him, "I have anointed you; I have called you. Go." And it came to pass.

We have what it takes inside because God placed it there, but the spirit of fear stops us, and we make excuses. It is not that we are not called, anointed or don't have potential. It is simply fear. But once you really trust God and discover that the God who created you has the blueprint of your life, your perspective will change. If you allow him to speak to your soul and follow his steps, you will be happy, because there is nothing like walking in God-given destiny and doing what he has called and gifted you to do.

I never knew I could teach and evangelize, but they were gifts placed in me. It took obedience to discover this. We are all able to minister. God wants your availability, not your power. Avoid fear and excuses at all costs.

It will not be your ability but God's power and might that change the world.

Conclusion

I want to invite you to take some time after reading these modern-day narratives to consider how God desires your partnership with his redemptive purposes. You can pray, you can give and you can go.

Sometimes our praying is our going, sometimes our giving is our going, but one thing is for certain — as followers of Christ, we are called to engage our world by going. We call those who travel to nations and to other cultures "missionaries." The reality in the Kingdom of God is that all who have been redeemed have this calling to live on mission, to go and make disciples. You can travel to far-away places and live on mission or you can stay right where you are because the mission of God is to reach people who are far away from him.

As I have traveled to many nations, I've realized the reason the early church continually prayed for boldness and courage is that it takes courage to follow God in every environment that people face. Courage is not the absence of fear, but facing your fears and overcoming those fears.

I've experienced this courage given by God in the tribal settings of South America; in Africa with Pastor Gacura having an open-air evangelistic meeting next to a mosque; in the villages of Asia with terrorists joining the gathering and listening to the Gospel; in Buddhist, Hindu and Muslim nations where proclaiming the Gospel of Christ brings harsh persecution. I have seen this boldness at work in home churches in closed communist nations and even in Washington, D.C., with Rob Schenck.

It doesn't matter if it's communism, consumerism, Buddhism, terrorism or any other kind of ism. What we need is a fresh outbreak of boldness and courage to believe Jesus and the power of his Gospel. The kind of courage that will jettison our fears so that we can declare it fearlessly.

If you have been compelled by the Holy Spirit to go to the nations, obey those promptings. If you are moved by the mission of God in your community, don't relegate it to others. Get involved with your voice, your hands and your feet.

If you have read these stories and realize you have lived your life far away from God, not knowing his forgiveness, love and grace, you can experience life transformation right now.

How does this transformation occur?

Recognize that what you're doing isn't working and that you have come short of the glory of God. Accept the fact that Jesus desires to forgive you for your bad decisions, selfish motives and sin. Realize that without this forgiveness, you will continue a life separated from God and his amazing love. In the Bible, the book of Romans, chapter 3, verse 23 reads: "For all have sinned and fall short of the glory of God." That's the bad news. The good

Conclusion

news we can read in Romans, chapter 6, verse 23: "The result of sin (seeking our way rather than God's way) is death, but the gift that God freely gives is everlasting life found in Jesus Christ." Eternal life instead of death is good news.

Believe in your heart that God passionately loves you and wants to give you a new heart. Ezekiel 11:19 reads: "I will give them singleness of heart and put a new spirit within them. I will take away their stony, stubborn heart and give them a tender, responsive heart" (NLT).

Believe in your heart that "if you confess with your mouth that Jesus is Lord and believe in your heart that God raised him from the dead, you will be saved" (Romans 10:9, NLT).

Believe in your heart that because Jesus paid for your failure and wrong motives, and because you asked him to forgive you, he has filled your new heart with his life in such a way that he transforms you from the inside out. Second Corinthians 5:17 reads: "When someone becomes a Christian, he becomes a brand new person inside. He is not the same anymore. A new life has begun!"

Why not pray now?

Lord Jesus, if I've learned one thing in my journey, it's that you are God and I am not. I want your will and not my will. My choices have not resulted in the peace I hoped they would bring. Not only have I experienced pain, I've also caused it. I know I am separated from you, but I want that to change. I am sorry. I repent and ask your forgiveness for the choices I've made that hurt myself and others and for denying you. I believe your death paid for my sins, and you are now alive to change me from the inside out. Would you please do that now? I ask you to come and live in me so that I can sense you are here with me. Thank you for hearing and changing me. Now please help me know when you are talking to me, so I can cooperate with your efforts to change me. Amen.

Declare it Fearlessly,
David Pepper

For more information about David Pepper and missionary opportunities, please contact him at:

Amazon Outreach
P.O. Box 873060
Wasilla, AK 99687

Phone: 907-376-4965
Cell: 907-841-2434
Davidandjoydrick@gmail.com
http://www.facebook.com/pages/amazon-outreach/645591388817621

For more information on the missionaries in this book, check out their Web sites:

Jack McKee: http://newlifebelfast.com/
http://www.facebook.com/jack.mckee.5

Dominic Russo: http://dominicrusso.com/
http://1nation1day.com/

Lindsay Russo: http://www.angelhouse.me/

David Eubank: http://www.freeburmarangers.org/

Canisius Gacura:
http://www.facebook.com/canisious.gacura

Reverend Rob Schenck: http://www.faithandaction.org/

Steven Mayanja: http://www.facebook.com/womf.org

For more information on reaching your city with stories from your church, go to www.testimonybooks.com.

GOOD CATCH
PUBLISHING

Did one of these stories touch you?
Did one of these real people move you to tears?
Tell us (and them) about it on our Facebook page at
www.facebook.com/GoodCatchPublishing.